Let Us Now Prais[illegible]men

Let Us Now Praise Famous Women

A Memoir

FRANK SIKORA

The University of Alabama Press   Tuscaloosa

The University of Alabama Press
Tuscaloosa, Alabama 35487-0380

Manufactured in the United States of America
Designer: Michele Myatt Quinn
Typeface: AGaramond

∞

The paper on which this book is printed meets the minimum requirements of American National Standard for Information Science–Permanence of Paper for Printed Library Materials, ANSI Z39.48-1984.

Library of Congress Cataloging-in-Publication Data

Sikora, Frank, 1936–
Let us now praise famous women : a memoir / Frank Sikora.
p. cm.
ISBN 0-8173-5148-5 (pbk. : alk. paper)
1. Helms family. 2. Sikora, Frank, 1936– —Family. 3. Sikora, Frank, 1936– 4. Whites—Alabama—Calhoun County—Social life and customs—20th century. 5. Journalists—United States—Biography. 6. Alabama—Social life and customs—20th century. 7. Alabama—Race relations. 8. Calhoun County (Ala.)—Social life and customs—20th century. 9. Calhoun County (Ala.)—Rural conditions. 10. Calhoun County (Ala.)—Biography. I. Title.
F330.S55 2004
976.1′63063′0922—dc22

2004011613

Let Us Now Praise Famous Women

1

When she died on that March day in 1989, the skies had exploded tons of rain. Yellow lightning flashed upside-down *Ys* in the sky; thunder roared angrily as though in salute to her fiery temper.

It was fitting weather to say farewell to Minnie Belle Helms.

Standing near the soggy mound of flowers after the funeral, I said, "Well, she was an ornery old lady, but I guess in a way I'll miss her."

My son-in-law, Johnny Carpenter, a tall, dark-haired man of thirty-four, shook his head slowly. "Not me. She was the meanest one person I ever knew."

He grinned slightly as he spoke, but I had to admit he was right. She was hardheaded, and it was clear from the first she was a segregationist (although by the end, you had to wonder about that). But we just never figured why she became so angry for no apparent reason.

Mrs. Helms and her husband, Dan, were my wife's parents. I first saw them on a hot summer afternoon thirty years before, on my first visit to Alabama.

In the withering heat of that August day in 1959 the old house was a portrait of poverty in the South: a weathered frame structure that sat on brick corner posts, the sides covered with whitish-gray shingles that were discolored with age. The roof was tin, with some of the edges curling up.

This was Wellington, a rural community in northeast Alabama, sitting off U.S. 431 between Anniston and Gadsden. It was home to about two hundred souls.

Two of them were sitting on the front porch. They glanced with detached interest as I pulled the blue Ford Fairlane to a stop on the dusty road. Dan and Minnie Belle Helms. She was sixty, he seventy.

She was on the swing, arms folded somewhat defiantly, mouth drawn tight, eyes narrowed behind the wire-rimmed glasses. Her hair, which had been a deep brown when she was younger, was now tinged with gray.

As we were getting out of the car, I glanced at my wife, Millie, who was obviously excited about being home. She was an outgoing woman with dark-brown eyes, a narrow, slightly upturned nose, and medium-length brown hair that had an auburn tint. She looked much younger than her twenty-seven years.

"Come on," she said. "I want you to meet my daddy and mom."

In that split second I could not picture her one day looking like her mother. But I didn't say anything.

Mr. Helms was seated in a wooden rocking chair. He was a burly man who wore faded green work pants, a plaid shirt, and, despite the heat, a rumpled, gray suit coat. A droopy, worn-slick brown hat covered his head, which it turned out, was bald with gray strands at ear level. He had a weary look about him, an expression that seldom changed. But the gray-green eyes showed warmth; and crinkles formed around them on those rare moments when he smiled.

Both had tanned faces that were braced with stern lines. I made these observations as we walked toward them through air that was so humid it was like wading in sweat.

Millie gave them a hug. Then she introduced me to them. They merely nodded, and I thought they seemed uneasy with a stranger from Ohio in their midst. They spoke little, a trait that was due more to the snuff they kept in their mouths than the fact that they were unsociable.

Mr. and Mrs. Helms flanked by granddaughters Debbie (our daughter), *left,* and Carolyn Sharpton, *right,* ca. 1970.

Finally, Mrs. Helms looked at me and in a monotone asked:

"Well, what are you?"

Puzzled, I shook my head. "What am I?"

She gave a brief "hmmp" sort of laugh, and her eyes twinkled. Then: "I mean are you a Yankee? Or a damn Yankee?"

Mr. Helms chuckled slightly but said nothing as he stared at the floor of the porch.

I shrugged. "I'm not sure. Is there a difference?"

"Well, I don't know," drawled Mrs. Helms, speaking slowly. "I always heard it said both ways and I was just a-wonderin' about it. I thought maybe you might tell us."

"I'm one or the other, I suppose," I said.

Now Mr. Helms tilted his head sideways, glanced up at me and muttered, "They got different meanings to 'em." A pause. Then: "A 'Yankee' is someone from up North who comes down here for a spell then goes back to where he come from. A 'damn Yankee' is one who comes down here and stays!"

And with that both of them chortled, the merriment strong enough to cause their shoulders to quake.

I nodded and joined their laughter. "I guess I'm just a Yankee."

At the time I was twenty-three. There was no way of knowing . . . but within a few years I was to become a damn Yankee.

There was a big water oak in the lawn. The leaves were wilted in the heat, but its shade kept the porch reasonably cool on such sultry days. Dust-covered hedges lined the front of the lawn. In the yard itself were several tires that served as small flower containers. Across the road were two sets of railroad tracks. About two-hundred yards to the east was a train station, a white frame structure with green trim. Trains ran from Birmingham to Atlanta twice a day, and sometimes at night, Mr. Helms informed me. Another set of tracks near the station ran north-south.

The interior of the house swam with the stale aroma of old furniture, worn linoleum, flour, coffee, and a big can of bacon grease that sat on a table near the stove. There were three small bedrooms, all lined up on the right side, running front to back. On the left side was the living room, the dining room (which they rarely used), and the kitchen.

In the first bedroom was a chest of drawers, its top loaded with little knickknacks, one of them a figure of a small black boy sitting on a commode. The words inscribed on it read, "You-r-next." There were also postcards, small oil lamps, and a statue of a circus horse.

At the back porch was a well. A bucket tied to a rope sat on top, and hanging on the side was a metal dipper. The water was so icy cold it took my breath away.

Mr. Helms said that he kept a few small fish in it to eat "the green stuff" that grew in the water. This bit of news, I might add, came after I had gulped down a dipper full.

There was no running water indoors and no bathroom. Out back, down toward the end of a garden, was the outhouse, an enduring monument to the poverty in the Deep South from the Civil War through the present. Did most people in Alabama live like this? I wondered.

They were buying the house for forty dollars a month. It was the first one they had ever owned. Their entire life had been spent in rented houses or sharecropper shacks, Millie told me. They had managed to make a down payment on this one the year before. It would be theirs in five more years.

There was a larger garden alongside the yard. Mr. Helms planted watermelons, corn, and okra there. In the back he had more corn, plus some greens and squash, both the yellow crookneck type and a green, hard-shelled autumn variety.

I was amazed to find that they survived on about $155 a month from Social Security and a World War I pension. Neither had a formal education, . . . but they could teach me some things about thrift and keeping up with what money you had.

That first visit in the summer of 1959 brought a strange fascination with the South, with Alabama, and with the poor folks there.

That initial visit was the first time I picked a watermelon from a home patch. And it was the first time I saw signs that read "White Only" or "Colored" at water fountains and other places.

2

In early March 1960 we returned to Alabama. The nation's interstate system was incomplete, and the ride from Columbus, Ohio, to Wellington took about sixteen hours, with a good portion of the time spent on the twisting, turning sections of U.S. 27 in the high hills of Kentucky and Tennessee. But seeing spring unfolding in Alabama was worth the ride. It was my favorite time to be there, and I soon learned it was the choice season for just about everyone. Even Mrs. Helms, who, I would soon learn, had an eruptive temper, said she enjoyed March and early April.

"They all right, I guess," she allowed. "But if a cloud comes up, then I don't care much for either of 'em."

When a cloud comes up in springtime, it means thunderstorms, and thunderstorms carry the prospect of tornadoes. One had swept through the community in 1954, and the memory of what nature could do had a deep impact on Minnie Belle and Dan Helms. As a constant reminder, there was a big pine tree on the edge of their property that had a two-foot length of sheet metal driven through it by the winds of the twister.

But on the day we rode into the state, spring was just breaking out. The array of colors ran into the horizon, a picture of peace and serenity: wisteria, forsythia, peach blossoms, and ankle-high purple-blue crocus graced farmlands and small towns alike. And in the woodlands there was a dazzling glow where the redbud trees bloomed, the colors ranging from a vibrant red to an almost purple shade. Dogwood blossoms of white and pink were a soft contrast to the leafless branches of the hardwoods. When we had left Ohio there was rain mixed with sleet. But Alabama was another world. However, I was told, March nights in Alabama can be chilly (in fact, I learned, it's more likely to snow in March than in December).

Down the road from the Helms house was a bright row of yellow daffodils that paraded along a faltering gray-white picket fence. Smaller trees and brambles had overgrown the interior of the place, but a stack of bricks marked where a fireplace had been. This had once been home for a family.

In my mind I could see Yankee troops riding by a century earlier, setting the place afire. But it turned out to be nothing quite so dramatic. Mr. Helms said a fire had destroyed it a few years before.

I asked him about it, and he mulled it over for a while, gazing at the old homesite.

"The folks had moved out," he said. "Then one night it caught fire. Don't know for sure what caused it. It happened a spell before we moved here. We was still out yunder a ways."

By then I had become accustomed to the eating habits of poor folks. Breakfast was usually biscuits (made with lard), thick-sliced bacon, and coffee. Lunch was biscuits or sausage and coffee. And supper was cornbread, butter beans or pinto beans, and sometimes fried potatoes, and, depending on the season, greens. They especially liked turnip greens in spring and again in the fall, and in the early spring there was something they called poke salat. I never did taste any of that.

We often ate at the home of Robert and Louise Sharpton. Louise, thirty-nine, was Millie's older sister. Sometimes their brother, James Helms, thirty-five, and his family would be there.

Those evening meals were often a thing to behold: there might be twelve to fifteen people either at the table or reaching over it with plates to ladle on some beans or grabbing for biscuits or cornbread, everybody talking at once.

Once a big dog named "Rounder" worked his way unnoticed

into the house and sort of wedged his way to the table, nabbing a piece of cornbread before anyone could stop him. Old Rounder was fast, all right.

"Get on out of here, sir!" grumbled Mr. Helms, swiping with a burly arm. "Go on now."

Rounder laid back his ears, lowered his tail, and backed away.

I'd never heard a dog addressed with the title of "sir."

And Robert, a lean man with straight, slicked-back brown hair, with only a glance from his plate, called in a toneless voice, "Louise, run Rounder on outa here."

She shooshed him out with a swipe of a dish towel. When that wasn't enough, she threatened to take the broom to him.

At first I wasn't much for butter beans. After all, I had been raised in middle-class Ohio, where we regularly had steak and potatoes, or pork chops, or ribs and sauerkraut. On Sundays my mother made Swiss steak with tomato gravy and big potatoes and onions roasted right in with it.

But when you get hungry, things can change. First time I ladled some butter beans onto a plate, I studied them for a moment.

Mr. Helms glanced at me and said, "Break you up some cornbread in it. Makes it taste better."

And Robert added, "Francis, cut you some onions up and mix 'em in. That makes it taste a whole lot better."

I tried both suggestions and found that it made a tasty dish, especially on a chilly night . . . and especially if you hadn't eaten all day. We ate fast. The time to slow down and talk came after the eating, when the young ones headed out to play and the adults could sit back and sip sweetened ice tea or coffee.

Robert was usually the first to complete his meal, finishing it off by dabbing a biscuit into what was left of the gravy. Then he set the plate aside, fetched a Camel cigarette from his pocket, and lighted it with his head tilted slightly downward. The whole thing was done in one deft motion. He told me he had started smoking when he was about twelve. He had served in World War II with the Sixth Infantry Division in the Pacific. He never talked to me about it much, other than to say he was picking cotton one day when someone brought him his notice from the draft board.

Although I adapted to the diet, the poverty was something that was not as easy to accept. It seemed to me the only pleasures the people had were tobacco—either snuff or cigarettes—and occasionally buying or baking a cake and having it with coffee. Often on cool spring days, when company came, they would sit on the porch and enjoy coffee. I remember my first look at the way some of the men drank it.

We were gathered on the front porch of the Helms house. Robert and James squatted and said little as they drew deeply on nonfiltered cigarettes. Louise brought Robert a cup of coffee and a shallow bowl or saucer. James was given the same. Between puffs on the cigarettes, they poured the coffee into the saucers, then sipped it. I had to wonder why they drank it that way.

On one of those days I first met Millie's uncle, Lee Shortnacy, a World War I vet who had spent time in France. He was in his early seventies, lean, and seemingly angry about everything. It was clear he had little use for me. When he was getting his coffee, I asked if he wanted any sugar or cream.

Without looking at me he growled, "I like real coffee."

He then commenced to sip his brew, black and unsweetened coffee, from the saucer.

Properly dressed down, I turned to Robert. "Why do you pour the coffee into the saucer? Why not drink it from the cup?"

He grinned slightly. "It tastes better from the saucer," he said, his voice low and husky. "Ain't that right, James?"

James narrowed his eyes, obviously giving the topic deep thought. Then he nodded. "Tastes better and it cools it down some." Then he looked at me. "Oughta try it sometimes. Don't you think so, Uncle Lee?"

It was an invitation for his views on coffee drinking, made for my benefit. But Uncle Lee didn't respond. He blew a puff of smoke out and glanced over at Robert. In a loud voice he announced, "Got me some new tires today. Them others was wearin' out."

Uncle Lee, like Robert and James, was a heavy smoker, also preferring Camels. When I offered him one of my filter-tipped menthols, he shook his head and muttered, "I like real cigarettes. Got no use for filters."

He didn't have any use for damn Yankees, either, it seemed.

So I stayed out of the way, sitting on the end of the porch, listening and observing. The afternoon faded into a cool evening.

Off beyond the old homesite where the daffodils grew, a whippoorwill's forlorn cry echoed in the gathering gloom. Other creatures answered, and soon there was a chorus of calls. We listened, saying little. Finally, Robert drawled, "Louise. Reckon it's time to go to the house. I gotta be at work by six in the mornin'."

"Well . . . let's get 'em all together," she replied.

Now Robert, who was forty-one, uncoiled from his squatting position. He stretched. He was a thin man with a heavily lined face, the wearing of time etched in each crease. He had been raised on Sand Mountain, a high ridgeline that runs from Gadsden to Chattanooga, Tennessee. As a boy, he had spent most of his time plowing fields behind a mule. When he wasn't plowing, he was picking cotton. Lighting another cigarette and snorting out a dual puff of smoke, he patiently intoned, "Louise. Ready?"

So now they all stood and moved slowly toward the steps, the youngsters giggling and reaching around the elders to slap at one another.

Then Robert spoke the words that were almost a ritual in these parts when it's time for a departure.

In a toneless voice, he drawled, "Y'all come go with us."

A pause: Then Mrs. Helms muttered wearily, "Y'all stay."

"Y'all come go with us," said James, as he led his group from the porch.

Again Mrs. Helms, one hand propped on her cheek, responded in a flat voice, "Y'all stay."

It occurred to me that none of them really meant it. It was just a formality. But it was something that was expected.

3

While we continued to live in Columbus, through the early 1960s, we went to Alabama about once a year, usually in spring. Millie liked Ohio, but there was never any doubt she had Alabama on her mind, especially in the winters. She yearned to be in the warm climates and even talked about moving to Florida. So, in March 1961, we headed for Port Charlotte, Florida, where, we were told, you could find a new house for about $12,000 and spend your days on the pristine beaches of West Florida. Getting a job would be no problem, a land agent told me.

Mr. and Mrs. Helms came along because they had never been there before. We drove all night, once taking the wrong road in Georgia, then finally heading south. We arrived in the central part of the state at dawn and were enveloped by the fragrance of oranges ripening in the orchards.

Millie was one of those people who trusted most of the advertisements she saw or read, and Mrs. Helms believed just about everything Millie told her. Those ads said things like, "Come to Florida and enjoy the golden sands, the golden sun, etc. etc."

Well, one night at a cheap motel near Port Charlotte was about all of golden Florida we could stand. Everyone awoke the next morning feeling tired, fussy, and ready to get back home.

We started back in the late morning cutting through a lingering mist that smelled like fresh-poured orange juice, thick and sweet. The aroma was everywhere. We were passing lush green groves that sprouted up on both sides of the highway.

Mrs. Helms kept saying how much she'd like to drive into one of the groves for a better look. I just couldn't get the hint. Finally, she blurted out, "Mildred, can't we just stop by one of these orchards and see if we can get us an orange? They just smell so sweet."

"Sure," Millie said. Then she instructed, "Frank, pull into one of these groves so Mother can see what they look like up close."

I glanced at her with alarm. "Pull in? We can't just pull into somebody's orange grove. It's private property."

Millie shook her head and smiled. "They don't care. They like tourists down here. That's why they don't have fences. You just don't know much about Florida."

I resisted, saying it would be trespassing—no matter how much they liked tourists. And besides, I added, they liked tourists who had money and were free with spending it. We did not fit into that category.

"Aw, just turn in," Mrs. Helms said. "We'll just stay a minute."

Her husband cautioned, "I don't believe we need to be goin' on other people's land."

Minnie's temper flared. "Well, durn it, Dan Helms! I ain't never seen oranges growin' on trees like this. I just want to see one."

"All right, all right," I said, hoping to avoid a fight in the car. "I'll turn in to the next one we come to. Mr. Helms, we might as well get this over with or we'll never hear the end of it."

About a quarter mile farther up the road there was another grove on the left. I swung the car slowly across the shallow ditch and in between the row of trees. Big yellow fruit hung in abundance.

"These are grapefruit, not oranges," I said with some sarcasm. "Is this okay? Or does it have to be an orange grove?"

We were now about thirty or forty yards into the grove, and I stopped. As I did, I turned to the backseat and—to my alarm—Mrs. Helms was reaching out the open window for a big grapefruit that was hanging about a foot from the car.

Her face had a strange, almost hypnotic glow about it. Her hands were perfectly framed around a huge yellow fruit.

Just then a horn blew and a pickup truck came bouncing through the orchard toward us. I froze.

"Minnie, watch it, don't!" Mr. Helms was urgently shouting. "Don't get it!"

Now aware of the truck, Mrs. Helms withdrew her hands.

The pickup lurched to a halt beside us. I expected some big brute with a shotgun to get out. But instead, a middle-aged woman alighted. She was a stocky red-faced woman, and she wore a cowboy hat. She looked tough.

"What're you doin' here!" she shouted.

"Nothing," I said. "We were just looking."

"Well, the highway's back there, mister," she barked, gesturing. "Now you hit it before I call the police."

"Yes, ma'am," I said. And I followed her instruction to the letter. As we eased out of the orchard I glared at Millie, then back at her mother. "I hope the two of you are happy now."

Both of them laughed, and Mrs. Helms said, "Mildred, I was this close to gettin' that grapefruit. I just wanted to see what it was like to pull one from the tree. That's all I wanted. I really didn't care nothin' about eatin' it."

"Well, we'll get one before we leave Florida," Millie assured.

"Oh, no we're not," I protested. "You can get an orange if you buy one somewhere, but that's the only way. We're not going into any more groves."

Millie shook her head. "You don't have to go in. I'll go. I'll walk in. There's always a bunch of oranges that are left on the ground. They won't mind if I pick some up."

So later that day, as evening was settling in, we pulled along the edge of a small side road next to a grove, and Millie ran in, carrying a sack. As we waited, a police car drove by, which raised our blood pressure. But she finally came out with a load of what turned out to be the best-tasting oranges I ever ate.

4

Millie must have inherited some of her brass from her mother. She was athletic and extremely competitive. She had attended Alexandria High School, a few miles south of Wellington. As a sophomore she had once grabbed a ruler from a teacher who was going to rap her hands for some offense. It had gained her a suspension for a day and gave her a reputation as a rebel.

After graduation in 1949 she entered nursing school at Anniston, completing the training three years later. She accepted a position in Bethesda, Maryland. There she met Paul Burke, who was stationed at a Navy base in Virginia. They married in 1955 and after his release from the service, they moved to his hometown, Columbus, Ohio. They had a daughter, Deborah, born in March 1956. Then, the following January, Paul was killed in an industrial explosion at a plant where he worked. He was twenty-two. With the insurance money Millie put a $10,000 down payment on a new house, which cost $21,000.

Meanwhile, I'd enrolled at Ohio State in 1953, then the next year had entered the Army for two years, getting out in October 1956. I met Millie in the spring of 1958 at a little party. In October of that year we were married. I was twenty-two, going to business college in the mornings and working for a Columbus printing company, Lea-Mar Press, in the afternoons. We lived on my GI Bill money and the earnings I got from my part-time job. Millie also worked part-time and received a Social Security check for Deb.

(The marriage, after such a short engagement, surprised my family, since I had always been a social wallflower. In 1953, when I was a senior at St. Benedict High School in Cambridge, Ohio, I wanted to ask Barbara Chlovechok to go to the prom. But I was afraid she'd turn me down, and I dreaded the humiliation. She was a beautiful girl, with honey-blond hair, but very shy and quiet. One day at noon, just after the lunch hour, I saw her sitting alone in the classroom. It was the chance I'd been waiting for. But at that moment Sister Rita Marie entered through another door. Panicked, I did an about-face and never said anything to her. Fifty years later, just before the class reunion in 2003, I told her about it. She said she would have accepted. In fact, she did go with me to the reunion, which was attended by eleven of the twenty grads.)

By March 1962, in addition to Debbie, who was then six, we had Victor, Frankie, and Terry. As Millie and I struggled to raise a family, I worked at various jobs, including selling parts at a Volkswagen warehouse, delivering baked goods, and even trying to be a door-to-door salesman. I desperately needed to find something that paid more.

I started trying to write, using a portable Smith-Corona typewriter Millie found at a pawn shop. After about thirty rejection letters, I managed to get a small article published in *Home Life* magazine, as well as a longer one in the *Columbus Dispatch Sunday Magazine.*

In April 1962 we returned to Wellington, with the idea of staying for a time and hoping I could find a job. Neighbors promised to keep an eye on the house. Driving to Alabama was getting to be a real struggle, with four small children.

By then, of course, I had found that not all people in Alabama were poor, and not all lived in houses without plumbing. In fact, Anniston and adjoining Oxford had street after street of nice homes and some that were described as luxurious. Some families had their own swimming pools, and many people lived in step with middle-class Americans everywhere.

But the state did have more than its share of very poor people who lived much like Millie's parents. For them, life went on much as it had in the Depression of the 1930s. The state also had a reputation for racial intolerance, which was displayed in dramatic style in May 1961. A racially mixed group of college students, calling themselves "freedom riders," had set out from Washington and planned to ride buses through the South. Their goal was to see if public facilities at bus stations were still segregated. Arriving in Anniston on May 14, Mother's Day, they had been met by a mob of white men, most of them members of the KKK. The mob threw objects at the bus, followed it out of the town, then stopped it, throwing a smoke bomb in through a window, setting it on fire. Meanwhile, a second bus went on to Birmingham. There the riders were beaten by another mob. The following Saturday, the same thing happened in Montgomery. President Kennedy sent U.S. marshals to the state and Governor John Patterson activated the National Guard to maintain order. It was the kind of thing that made national news and made outsiders wonder if they wanted to visit the state.

Regardless, we returned in that spring of 1962. The race for governor was going on, and I was to see some old-fashioned campaigning, as Democrats were to hold their primary in May. Alabama, at the time, was a one-party state: Democratic. The Republicans hardly bothered to run, as the party was still strongly associated with Abraham Lincoln, the Civil War, and Reconstruction.

On Saturdays Mr. and Mrs. Helms, and their older daughter, Louise, and her family, would ride into Anniston and spend much of the day "just looking around." That's all they could afford to do. "Going to town" was a tradition among many Alabama families. And they would do it for hours. (Black families did the same thing on Saturdays. And in rural areas if they didn't go to town, the women would often gather at a neighbor's house to visit. They referred to it as "going to society.") After one such trip, walking around the stores in Anniston, I decided I would rather work in Mr. Helms's garden, or spend time by the burned-out homesite, throwing rocks at trees.

One day Millie asked me to go into Anniston to pick up some milk for the baby and some other items. Mr. Helms decided he would ride with me. As he got into the car, he muttered, "Don't know if I oughta ride with you or not."

I gave him a quizzical look. "Why is that?"

"You got this Ohio tag on your car," he said. Then, after a pause, he added, "Some Klan folks liable to think I'm a damn Yankee, too."

I glanced over at him, slightly alarmed. "The Klan?"

Then his face rippled into a rare smile. He waved a hand forward. "Go on. Let's get to town."

We rode into Anniston and nothing happened, although I kept glancing into the rearview mirror. But the fact of the matter was that no one seemed at all interested in a car with an Ohio tag. In fact, it was pointed out to me that a lot of the soldiers at nearby Fort McClellan were from the North, and they had not encountered trouble with the KKK.

A few days later, Mr. Helms again rode with me to Anniston to buy some things. It was a cool and pleasant spring day. After parking the car, I heard a chorus of shouts and cheering.

"What's going on?" I asked.

He shook his head. Then, with contempt in his voice, he snorted, "Some of them politicians, I reckon. They runnin' for governor."

The noise was coming from about a block away. "Sounds like a big crowd," I said. "Let's go see what it's all about."

He stopped and gazed toward the sounds, his face perplexed. It was clear he didn't want to spend time at a rally when there were things we had to do. Finally, he said, "Well, I reckon we can go there for a spell. But we can't be gone too long; she'll pitch a fit."

"Who?"

He glanced at me as though I was deranged.

"Whata you mean 'who'? Minnie, that's who," he growled. "She gets mad if I stay too long somewheres. Real mad."

"We won't stay long," I assured him.

We hurried on and soon came to the Calhoun County Courthouse, a red-brick structure with a white tower. In front of it was a sight I had never beheld: a crush of humanity pressed up to a flatbed truck that served as a stage. There were Confederate flags flying both on the flatbed and in the hands of the audience, which appeared to be under a spell.

Just as we reached the outer perimeter a bluegrass band struck up "Dixie," and the throng erupted into an ear-splitting roar, punctuated with rebel yells. Then they clapped, keeping time with the melody. As we passed by the edge, some of the people, smiling and clapping their hands, paused to give us a pat on the back. They viewed us as fellow supporters, I supposed.

It was an awesome, yet eerie, feeling, like stepping back into a history book. This must have been close to the mood that prevailed in Montgomery when Alabama seceded 101 years before, I thought. In the back of my mind a voice was saying, "You should be writing about this."

Then I shouted to Mr. Helms, "I've never seen anything like this in Ohio."

He nodded. "Big crowd." Then he added, "It was like this back yunder. Big crowds."

"Back yunder" meant back in the 1930s and 1940s, I figured.

But this was 1962. The crowd now was for a candidate named George C. Wallace, a short, dark-haired middleweight with a heavyweight voice. His appearance onstage was what had set off the tumultuous welcome. He went to the microphone and, after a slow start, exploded with a verbal attack on the government in Washington. He kept one hand in his side pocket; the other flailed as he raged about "carpetbaggin' federal judges" and President John Kennedy, as well as Attorney General Robert Kennedy.

He also railed about attempts to desegregate schools and boasted about "keeping our way of life."

The crowd reacted with each point. I glanced about and noticed there was not a single black person in the audience. Later I saw several standing down the street, a block or so away.

"I wish I had something to write with," I said.

Mr. Helms felt in his shirt pockets, then gave a futile shrug. "Ain't got nothin'."

Wallace continued his tirade. I wanted to listen to more of it, but Mr. Helms tugged at my elbow and said we had to go. He again said something about Mrs. Helms getting sore if he stayed gone too long.

Dan Helms was a muscular man, strong as a bull, even though he was over seventy. But he did his utmost to avoid riling his wife. And for good reason. I was to discover soon enough that she had a temper as violent as a March thunderstorm. It appeared suddenly . . . and there wasn't always an apparent reason for it. It just exploded.

We left the rally then, but I kept looking back. I had never heard of George Wallace until that day. And even though I was not a seasoned political reporter, it didn't take much political savvy to realize that this man was going to be the likely winner, and with racial discord running high in Alabama, he would be a force to be reckoned with.

"You think he's going to win?" I asked Mr. Helms.

He shook his head slowly. "Naw. He won't beat Big Jim Folsom."

Turned out, of course, that Dan Helms was wrong. Wallace did win. And the troubles in the Deep South grew with the passing time, much of it a result of his win. I hasten to add that Wallace couldn't be blamed for all the troubles in the South.

But seeing that rally only sharpened my desire to get into journalism somehow. A day later I returned to Anniston and went to the local newspaper, the *Anniston Star.* I was twenty-six at the time and needed to get into a career with a future, something I liked.

I walked into the *Star,* filled out an application, and was taken to editor Cody Hall.

After giving my name, I added quickly, "I'm from Ohio."

"We won't hold that against you," he shot back, laughing.

But he didn't hire me. There was one slot open, he told me; and one of the candidates had a master's degree in English from the University of North Carolina.

5

My first experience with Minnie Belle Helms's temper came one morning shortly after the Anniston visit. I was in the living room, and she was in the kitchen preparing breakfast. Mr. Helms was with her. Millie was getting the children dressed in the bedroom.

Suddenly Mrs. Helms cried out angrily, "Durn, durn! Git out before I knock the fire out of you! Go on, git!"

At first I thought she might be yelling at one of the dogs that hung out in a loosely wired compound by the side rear of the house. But it wasn't one of them. Mr. Helms came shuffling out through the dining room and into the living room, his face grim, his eyes narrow and dull.

"What's wrong?" I asked. A survival instinct told me to keep my voice low.

Millie had come out of the bedroom and raised her hand to shush me. I followed my father-in-law onto the front porch and repeated the question.

"Aw, she's in there raisin' sand," he muttered. Then he turned his head quickly to make sure she might not hear.

"What'd you do?" I asked, perhaps a bit too nosy.

He shrugged. "Said something about the biscuit dough."

"The biscuit dough?" I shrugged in bewilderment. "What'd you say?"

He let out a long sigh. "Asked if it was about ready to bake. She gets mad when I say anything. Blows up over nothin'."

When breakfast was ready, we went to the kitchen—quite cautiously, I might add—and ate, consuming the coffee and homemade biscuits without a word. Mrs. Helms glowered at us for a moment or two, then retired to the bedroom, saying she had a bad headache.

Trying to ease the tension, Millie softly remarked, "Good tasting biscuits, aren't they?"

I shook my head. Then in a wretchedly weak voice, I said, "Durned if I'm going to say anything one way or the other."

As soon as we had finished, Mr. Helms jumped up and began washing the dishes. I pitched in. I didn't want to have Mrs. Helms come in and hit the roof again. But before we finished she did return, took a Goody powder, then went back to the bedroom.

Several hours later, as I stood in the road and threw rocks at a tree, Mr. Helms came out and watched, occasionally casting glances back toward the house.

"Has she always been like that?" I asked. "Just blowing up over nothing?"

He didn't answer, just nodded, again stealing a quick glance at the house.

For ten or fifteen minutes I kept tossing rocks. Finally Mr. Helms, who seemed to regain his composure, slapped me on the arm.

"Want to hear a good story?" he asked, his voice low.

I hesitated, thinking it might be about Negroes. But finally I shrugged and nodded. "Yeah, okay."

Another quick look at the house to make sure no one was in hearing distance, then he said:

"This fella wanted to have his cow serviced. So he took it over to this farm where the man had a big stud bull. Well, when he gets there the lady of the house answers the door. So—"

"This a true story?" I interrupted.

Mr. Helms nodded, the smile broadening. "Anyway, the fella says to the lady, 'Your husband home?' And she says he ain't home. Well, that kind of set him back and he says, 'Reckon I'll come back later.' And the woman says, 'Can I help you with somethin'?' "

Before he could go on, Mr. Helms started chuckling then and I started laughing, knowing the punch line was probably drawing near. He continued:

"Well, he didn't know what to say, so he says to her, 'No, I'll come back.' Well, the lady says, 'You need that cow serviced?' His face turns red as a beet and he says yeah. So she says, 'Bring her back by the barn.' So he takes her back there by the barn. And the lady, she brings that bull out. But he don't do nothin'. That bull just stands there."

Mr. Helms has to stop, as laughter seems to consume him. He has tears in his eyes, he has been laughing so hard. Then, slapping me on the shoulder, he struggles on:

"So the man says, 'I'll just come back later.' She says, 'No, just wait a minute.' And she goes and gets a big cob of that Tennessee Red corn and goes behind the bull and commences to rub him with the cob. Pretty soon that bull goes and mounts that cow. Well, the man starts laughin'. And the woman looks at him real mad, and she says, 'Are you laughin' at me, sir?' And he says, 'Oh, no, ma'am, I ain't laughin' at you. I was just thinkin' if my wife saw that, she'd get her a big corncob and rub my ass raw!"

Just before finishing the punch line Mr. Helms's chuckling broke into quivering laughter, and he again slapped me on the shoulder several times.

He kept talking: "You can just see his old lady chasin' him with a corncob."

I laughed. "Pretty good story."

It was a true story he assured me. There were others, and he was good at spinning a yarn.

Then, I asked, "Do you ever have anything to do with the Negro people who live down the road there?"

He glanced over the railroad tracks, which curved to the east, rolling toward Atlanta. Up on the embankment above the rails was a house with green tarpaper on the sides and a tin roof. There were several children playing in the yard.

"We get along," he said finally. "They usually just stay over there, and we stay here. Sometimes we see one another. They good people. We get along fine."

I nodded. "What's their name?"

Mr. Helms thought for a moment, then shrugged. "Durn if I can place it right now. I've heard before but I can't place it." Another pause. Then, shaking his head, he muttered, "I just can't get it right now. But they good folks."

"That's what's important," I said.

"But I swear I don't know what makes some of them want to go to school with white young-uns, and be at places with white folks," he muttered. "Seems to me they'd be better off bein' with their own kind." He spit tobacco juice, shook his head, then went on. "It ain't the coloreds around here that are stirrin' things up. It's them ones up in Washington and up North. Them and the damn Yankees."

"How do you feel about what's going on?" I asked.

He shrugged. "I believe in treatin' folks right, no matter what color they are. But I believe the Bible says there ain't to be no mixin' and such."

Later that day, when we were sitting on the front porch, he asked his wife, "Minnie, what's that colored woman's name that lives over yunder?"

"Why you want to know that for?" she asked.

Mr. Helms nodded at me. "He was asking."

"Why you need to know?" she asked, a touch of humor in her voice. Then, before I could answer, she said, "Rosie Woods is her name. Don't see a lot of her, but she's a good person. Most of the colored folks around here are. Some are sorry, but most are good."

"But you don't visit, that sort of thing," I said.

She shrugged. "I don't have no reason to go down there. And I guess they don't have no reason to come up here. If I did, and if they did, then I reckon we would each go to the other's house. But if there ain't no need to, then we don't. We ain't much for socializin' nohow. But I got nothin' against colored folks. They got their ways, and we got ours. That's the way I see it."

6

I'd often watch the children as they played outside, and to pass the time I'd throw rocks at trees. Men never cease being boys at heart. I'd make a game of it. If I hit a tree with a rock it was a completed pass. Get five in a row and it was a touchdown. But throwing rocks doesn't pay the milk bill. So after a few more days in Alabama, we headed back to Ohio. There I found a job driving a bread truck.

The fall came, followed by a harsh winter. Millie and our oldest child, Deb, then seven, contracted pneumonia. For Millie that winter was the last one she wanted to spend in Ohio. She told me she would like us to move to the South. She had a friend in Jacksonville, Florida, who said there was a need for nurses, and jobs in other areas were plentiful.

So in April 1963, when Birmingham, Alabama, was seething in civil rights marches and Police Commissioner Eugene "Bull" Connor was hosing down demonstrators, we began our journey. I was about to become a damn Yankee for sure. We stayed in Wellington for a few days, then drove on to Jacksonville. I failed to find a newspaper job and found little else. Our slim savings account soon ebbed, and by late summer we were in a crucial financial situation. By then the creditors were hounding us about the Chevrolet station wagon—we were three months behind—and my mind-set was in a state of siege mentality.

Meanwhile, I had put in for a job with the city of Jacksonville Beach. I'd take anything, I said.

On a Sunday morning in September I was trying to fix the kids some grilled cheese for lunch. The radio was on, and the news came on from the Mutual network. The lead story was about a bombing in Birmingham that killed four black girls.

I called to Millie, who was in another room and told her the news. She was stunned by the report. "Today?" she asked.

"Right during church," I said. "They killed four girls."

Standing in the doorway she lit a cigarette and stared at the floor. "Just kids," she said in disbelief. "They need to find who did it and hang them all."

"That'll be the day," I said. "They don't have to look farther than the Ku Klux Klan."

"The Klan is a lot stronger than you know," she said. "I've seen their parades in Anniston when I was in high school. It's like they owned the world."

We had planned to drive to Wellington for a visit, and the next morning we left. It meant driving through the near-downtown of Jacksonville. I was glad we didn't leave Sunday night. As we passed through the city that morning, we were surprised to find a scene of shattered store windows, rocks and bricks in the streets, broken bottles, and clusters of black people gathered at street corners. Some of them yelled as we rode by.

"Why are they doing that?" Debbie asked. The younger children didn't comprehend.

"Someone bombed a church in Birmingham and killed four little Negro girls," Millie explained. "I can imagine they are mad about that. It looks like they had a riot."

When we arrived in Wellington that afternoon, the talk was of family matters and the weather. After supper that night we sat up and watched the news on TV. Following the report of the bombing, Mr. Helms shook his head. "That's awful, young-uns being killed like that. No one had a right to do that, no matter what the colored folks had done."

Millie replied, "Daddy, they hadn't done anything. They were in church."

He shook his head. "I know, but earlier they had been marchin' and carryin' on about I don't know what. Back in the spring. Y'all remember."

"Well, ain't nobody got a right to bomb a church," Mrs. Helms declared. "I don't care if it is a colored church. They had no business. These colored folks out here go to church every Sunday and sometime during the week, and don't bother nobody."

We went back to Jacksonville Beach after several days, and the year that had gone wrong continued to do so. One morning a man and woman showed up at the door and curtly asked for the keys to our station wagon. They drove off in it. The same day the mortgage company called to say our house payment was three months behind and they were going to foreclose if we didn't do something quickly. In October a hurricane named Ginny was roaring up the Atlantic coast, the eye about one hundred miles east of Jacksonville Beach. I had to go to the store pulling a wagon to haul the few groceries we could afford. As if there wasn't enough personal worry, the television set went out. There was sound but no picture.

It had never occurred to me that television could somehow be more vivid without a picture, but I learned that fact on the twenty-second day of November 1963.

Debbie, who was seven, was outside playing with a friend. The other kids were romping about in a back room. Millie was in the garage, where we kept the washer and dryer. The front door opened and Debbie said, "Do you know President Kennedy?"

Puzzled by the question, I shrugged. "Do I know him? In a way. I know about him. Why?"

Her expression was solemn and perplexed. "Somebody shot him," she said simply. "It's on TV."

I hurried to the television set and turned it on, watching the blank screen. Then Walter Cronkite's voice—strained, breaking at times—could be heard.

"And then came the word that, indeed, the president was dead."

I shook my head in disbelief. It had to be a history special or something about Lincoln's assassination. It couldn't be real. But Cronkite continued, telling about Kennedy's arrival that morning and the motorcade through downtown Dallas. . . . Shots were heard . . . and the president's car was seen speeding to Parkland Hospital, where he died.

For four days we barely slept, staying in front of the blank television listening to the incredible developments: the Marine Corps' band playing a dirgelike version of "Hail to the Chief" . . . the muffled thumping of drums mixed with the clip-clop of horses' hooves along Pennsylvania Avenue . . . the bugler muffing the high note in "Taps." We didn't see it, but we visualized it, and it burned in our minds a vivid picture of the events.

It seemed the life of the nation had came to an abrupt halt. I went outside on the night of Kennedy's funeral and stared up at the stars and a pale quarter moon. Even they seemed sad. It was now a different world. I decided that night we had to leave Florida. I didn't know why. We just had to.

7

In January 1964 we scraped up enough money to buy train tickets. We went back to Alabama. Mrs. Helms greeted us with a cold silence but did give a brief nod. Mr. Helms also said nothing, but he gave the children a hug.

A snowstorm had hit the state on New Year's Eve, and there were still some splotches of white dashed under the rows of brown, rattling corn stalks. It was cold, the kind of cold that makes people hunch their shoulders to ward off the chill. But it was away from Florida, and it was good to be back. It wasn't really home, but it was the closest thing we had to one.

That night Mr. Helms sat in his rocking chair watching the news from Channel 6 in Birmingham. He wore his coat and hat, and he had the small gas heater on, the only source of heat in the house. The newsperson commented on the wintry conditions, saying, "It may be several more days before the weather moderates."

I had been standing in the doorway behind Mr. Helms. When there was a break for a commercial, I entered the living room and sat down. "Anything new?"

He shook his head wearily, then declared, "I wish this weather would moderate."

For the next several weeks I tried to find a job but had no luck. We were running up a hefty milk bill from the delivery man, who reminded me one morning that he'd like to be paid.

Finally the arctic air drifted away, and the air mellowed into springlike days; before long, daffodils gave a yellow glow to the sagging picket fence that marked the adjoining property.

But in contrast, with each passing day, Mrs. Helms seemed to grow more irritated by my presence. One day as I sat in the little dining room, trying to write a story on the portable typewriter, she fumed:

"You need to forget that newspaper stuff and messin' with that typewriter and get a real job." Her voice quivered with rage. "I oughta toss that durn thing away."

I said nothing, and Millie came to the rescue, urging her mother to sit on the porch with her.

Meanwhile our mail, which was being forwarded, carried a note from the City of Jacksonville Beach, Florida, which was in need of police officers. I figured I might try out for that. We decided to ride down and find out about it. As far as we knew, the house was still unoccupied. We had not heard from the mortgage company.

We bought a 1950 Dodge from Robert, who gave us a good price: $50. It had four bald tires, rusted spark plugs, and a muffler with a big hole in it. Somehow, it started.

One stormy evening in March 1964 we headed down U.S. 431, bound for Florida. We left against the wishes of Millie's sister, Louise, who feared tornadoes. She had a feeling about bad weather.

Flashes of lightning made the thunderheads look like dark dragons in the sky. The wind was humming from the southwest, making the car sway as we plowed through the rain; twigs and small branches blew across the road.

About sixty miles into the trip, south of the town of Wedowee, I heard a loud wailing sound and the car lurched to one side. A blowout! I was afraid it would happen, and it did.

Ahead, through the downpour, I saw the blurred glare of lights. A store. It would be a place to get off the road and change the tire. I limped along the final hundred yards and pulled into the small gravel parking area. It was one of those old country stores, a white-frame building with a front porch and two gasoline pumps out front.

Several men stood on the porch, observing us. They wore plaid shirts and blue work pants; two of them had hats tilted slightly to the side.

By now, the rain had slacked off slightly and I opened the door. Just as I did, there was a loud SWOOSH! as another tire blew. What incredible luck, I thought. The men stood silently, watching.

I went to the porch, not caring that I was getting slowly soaked.

"You got any used tires?" I asked.

The man in the middle, the one without the hat, and the apparent owner, nodded. "Got some used ones. Don't know if they're the right size or not."

By now the children, who had been sleeping, were awake. Millie got out of the car and took them inside to get some snacks. I warned her not to spend much.

The owner's wife stood behind the cash register. "Evening," she said. "Rough out. We're fixin' to close."

"We may wait a little," the man interceded. "He's got two flat tires."

"Well, I swaney," she said. "Two of them. And on a night like this."

I hurriedly looked over the few used tires and found two that were useable. "How much?"

He gazed down at them for a moment. "I'll let you have 'em for four dollars each."

I glanced at Millie. That was $8. We had figured it would take $15 for gasoline and food to get to Jacksonville Beach (gasoline was 33 cents a gallon then). We had about $30 with us. There was no choice.

"We'll take them," I said.

The owner nodded. He was a slim, graying man of about sixty or so. He wore dark-rimmed glasses. He glanced at the kids who were rummaging through the potato chip bags.

"Young man," he said finally, "where is it you're trying to go to tonight?"

"Jacksonville, Florida."

"Where'd you come from?"

"Just north of Anniston," I said.

He glanced at the other men, then back to me. "Well, it's none of my business," he said slowly. "But on a night like this, with all those kids and your wife with you, I think it would be a better idea just to turn around and go back up by Anniston. That's sixty miles. That'd be better than trying to drive three-hundred miles to Florida. Especially on those tires."

By now it was well after eleven o'clock, and I knew the store owners were eager to leave and go home. I pulled the lug wrench hard, tightening the last nut. Then I thanked the man and his wife.

The kids were in the back sleeping. I was drenched, cold, tired, and hungry. When I got inside I shook my head. I glanced over at Millie.

"Somebody or Something doesn't want you to go to Florida," she said, following up with a nervous laugh.

There hadn't been much to laugh about that night.

"Should we turn around?" I asked her.

"Yeah. I think we better."

We drove back into Wedowee, found a small restaurant open, bought two Styrofoam cups of coffee—bitter but hot—then continued north on U.S. 431.

"Your folks aren't going to like this," I said. "I think they've about had it with us."

She nodded. "Maybe we can stay with Louise and Robert for a while."

We stopped at a service station that was closed for the night and slept for a while. By then, the thunder and screaming winds had abated, and there was only a gentle rain. Later, we continued on and arrived back in Wellington at dawn. As we came to a stop, we saw Robert squatting down on the front porch, a cigarette dangling from his mouth. He held a cup of coffee in one hand, a shallow saucer in the other.

He glanced at us without emotion, although we could only imagine his disappointment at seeing us so soon.

When we walked up to the porch, he remained motionless, drawing on the cigarette. He nodded and muttered, "Howdy." Then, after a pause, "There's some coffee in the kitchen. Go get you some."

Robert worked in a food warehouse in Gadsden, although he was sometimes sent to Anniston, and usually awoke about 4:30 each morning. He had to be at work by 6:15. We went inside the house. Louise was up, stirring about in the kitchen.

She said nothing as we entered. But when she looked at us, her eyes twinkled slightly.

"We didn't make it to Florida," Millie announced in a matter-of-fact voice.

"I see you didn't," Louise said, as she prepared to make biscuits. "I didn't like y'all goin' out in such weather in the first place."

"We had two flat tires," Millie declared. "Can you believe that?"

"Well," Louise drawled slowly. "I guess somebody was telling y'all not to go back to Florida."

A short time later she produced a platter full of hot biscuits from the oven. As she put them on the table, she remarked, "I'm just glad y'all came back."

Later in the morning Mr. and Mrs. Helms showed up. Mrs. Helms appeared in an ill mood, and I assumed—correctly, I'm certain—it was because of our rapid return to Wellington.

8

One day in March the air was sticky and warm, the sun shone through rapidly moving clouds that were driven by a steady southwest wind. Then we heard thunder rumbling in the distance. Moments later, Louise pulled up out front in a green Ford station wagon.

"Let's go, Momma!" she called, her voice crackling with urgency.

"Where we a'goin'?" asked Mrs. Helms, peering at her through the screen door.

"Down by Robert's workplace," Louise called. In the distance another burst of thunder rumbled over the land. "Hurry, Momma."

I asked Millie, "Where are they going?"

"Anywhere but here," she answered. "Louise don't like to stay here when the weather turns bad. She's real scared of tornadoes."

The sky was alive with movement; dark-gray clouds spilled along in a tumbling, raucous pattern.

James, a short, slim fellow with dark-brown hair worn in a crew cut, had dropped by for a visit. He stepped outside and studied the clouds, his forehead wrinkled with worry. "Louise, you might oughta just stay here," he said. "One place ain't no safer than the other. You can't tell where one might hit. You don't want to be out on the road in this kind of weather."

James had been drafted into the Army in World War II and had been given a medical discharge after he began having nightmares of German soldiers coming to kill him. Millie was twelve or so at the time. She remembered going to Fort Jackson, South Carolina, with her parents and Uncle Lee to bring him home. The way he stared at the clouds gave me pause to wonder if he wasn't seeing things in the sky that the rest of us missed.

But Louise was hell-bent on going to Robert's workplace at a grocery warehouse in Anniston. She felt safer there, she said.

So the Helmses and Millie and our daughter, Deb, who was eight, and sons, Victor, Frankie, and Terry (five, four, and two), crammed into the station wagon along with Louise's children, Joyce, Jimmy, Carolyn, Jerry, and Patsy; and away they went, the station wagon emitting a burst of black smoke as Louise floored it in a desperate move to go someplace . . . anyplace.

I glanced at James and shook my head in puzzlement. I hadn't yet been introduced to the fear that a tornado can bring. A crack of lightning sent us indoors. The wind howled and torrents of rain whipped the house like bullets. Then it calmed down. A short time later the station wagon pulled up in front; Louise hurried out of the vehicle and strode to the house. Her face was white, her eyes reflecting fear.

"Everything all right?" I asked.

She didn't respond. Mrs. Helms came next, muttering, "Lord, Lord, have mercy."

With some trepidation, I asked, "What happened?"

She didn't answer. But Mr. Helms was behind her, carrying one of the younger children. He gazed at me like he had never seen me before.

"We went down the road," he said. "Got down yunder a ways and durn if a tornado don't pass right in front of us down the road. It crossed right in front of us."

I shook my head in disbelief. "You almost drove into a tornado?"

"Another quarter mile and we'd have been in it," Millie called. "All I saw was this black cloud tumbling along. I hollered at Louise to stop. Boy, she slammed on the brakes. She's a nervous wreck. We all are."

The children, luckily, were too young to realize the danger that they had barely eluded. In my mind it raised the question James had asked before: where do you run to? And is there a point to running at all?

One evening after supper, two of the children had a disagreement over toys. Terry, our son, and Patsy, Louise's daughter, both two, took a slap at each other. It brought Mrs. Helms scrambling from the kitchen table.

"Who hit Patsy?" she demanded.

Robert, who was seated in a corner chair, had watched the whole thing. Laughing, he related the events, adding that Terry had merely duplicated what had been done to him. "He didn't hit her hard at all," he said. "They both just hit at one another. It was nothing."

But that didn't satisfy Mrs. Helms. In an angry voice she cried out, "I'll tear that young-un up. I'll teach him to hit her."

At that point I picked up Terry and held him away from her. Things were getting out of hand.

She became enraged. "Give that boy to me," she ordered harshly.

"You're not going to hit him," I said. "He's just a child. Nobody was hurt."

She glared at me. "I said give him to me."

I didn't want to be involved in an argument with her, so I went out the front door and walked to the road.

Behind me I could hear her shouting angrily. A few minutes later Mr. Helms came out to the road. His face was unsettled. He shook his head slowly. "It ain't gonna do for you to come back to the house," he said.

I nodded. "Okay. I won't come back."

"It ain't me," he said. "It's her. She's mad as a hornet."

"I know. I know how she is. But I couldn't let her hit him. He's not even three yet."

Mr. Helms shook his head slowly. "I don't reckon she'd really hit him. But I don't blame you."

So after that we stayed with Robert and Louise in their crowded little brown house. It was one of the prefabricated structures. They owned several acres of land on both sides of the road. Out back they had some chickens and geese, and across the road there was a sizable garden. We slept on the living room floor. And Terry and Patsy were playing again on the floor, blithely unaware of the hornet's nest they had innocently stirred up.

After a few weeks, we found a house to rent. Millie and the children would sometimes go to see her parents at their home, but it would be more than a year before Mrs. Helms spoke directly to me.

9

In April 1964 Louise saw an ad in the Sunday edition of the *Anniston Star* for a dairy-farm worker. She showed it to Millie, who passed it along to me. The ad said the man picked for the job would have access to a small house on the farm property, and his family could have free milk. It provided a small wage.

"You have to apply at the State Employment Office in Gadsden," she said.

I nodded. Robert would be able to give me a ride into town, since he had transferred there a short time before from the Anniston warehouse.

So that Monday morning, April 27, I got up at 4:30, washed up in the kitchen, put on a pair of clean khaki pants and a short-sleeve plaid shirt, and walked to Robert's house. He had told me to be there by 5:15. It was a cool, misty morning. In the distance a train whistle wailed, and roosters announced the beginning of a new day.

Well, I thought as I walked along, my dreams of writing, of being a newspaper reporter were over. I was going to be a poor farmworker in the Deep South. I would wear dirty clothes, eat cornbread and beans, and probably earn enough to buy a pack of Camels every few days. And I would probably start sitting on the porch floor and drink coffee from a saucer.

Robert said little as we drove north along U.S. 431. Gadsden was not quite twenty miles away. He stopped the car along the main drive, called Meighan Boulevard, and let me out. It was 5:45 a.m.

"You know where the employment office is?" I asked.

He nodded to the left. "It's up there on Broad Street. You'll find it."

Then he drove off. It was dawn. The streetlights were on. The streets themselves were deserted. I walked the two blocks to Broad Street and found the employment office. It opened at 8:30. Well, I thought, I only have two hours or so to wait. I didn't see any restaurants open, which really didn't matter. I was flat broke.

So I stood in front of the building and waited. At least I would be first in line. The sun began to rise, a pink orb lifting into the cool mist that hung over the high hills to the east.

Gadsden seemed like a fairly nice city. I had been told that about sixty thousand people lived there. It was a steel town. But Goodyear Tire and Rubber also had a big plant there.

Down the street a block away was a blue sign that read the *Gadsden Times.* There was no use going there, I thought. They would never hire me. No, I was going to be a dairy-farm worker. Then I saw a light come on in the newspaper office. There was a big window in front, and I observed a man walking about in the office.

It was now 6:30. Time was dragging along. Then, around 7 a.m., I saw an old man walking along the street, coming toward me. He was gray-haired, wore glasses, and used a cane. As he drew nearer, he stopped for a moment and gazed at me.

"What you waitin' for?" he rasped.

I gestured toward the employment office. "Waiting for them to open."

Now he smiled, not a friendly smile, but a cat-and-mouse kind of smile.

"You got a long wait," he cried.

"I know," I said, without looking at him. I was in no mood for a long conversation. "It opens at eight-thirty."

Quickly the man hissed, "Eight-thirty tomorrow morning."

I stared at him in disbelief. "Tomorrow morning! What do you mean?"

"Today's a state holiday," he said, chuckling.

"Holiday." I was puzzled. "What holiday?"

He leaned forward, threw his chin out a little farther, and proudly proclaimed, "It's Confederate Memorial Day!"

And with that he went on his way, his gait noticeably more jaunty.

I was stunned. Confederate Memorial Day? I didn't even know such a day existed. Now what? I thought. Here I was at seven in the morning, and nowhere to go. I started a slow walk back toward Meighan, which was also U.S. 431. I would have to thumb a ride back to Wellington.

Now, inside the *Gadsden Times,* I saw two people moving about. Without thinking I went to the front door. It was unlocked. I walked in.

A woman was seated at the desk nearest the front door. She glanced up at me, appearing surprised that someone would come in this early.

"May I help you?" she asked.

"Yes, ma'am, I was looking for a job."

"A job? What kind of job?"

"A reporter," I said.

The woman (I later learned her name was Mary Hoffman) studied me curiously. Here I was in khaki pants and plaid shirt. This was 1964. Most male reporters—or those who wished to become journalists—dressed in sport coats and slacks and wore ties.

"Well," she said, with some hesitation, "You'll have to talk to the editor. He should be in shortly. If you'd like to have a seat."

I nodded and sat down on the small couch that was placed by the large front window. Presently a man in a tan raincoat entered the room. He went into the office that had the words "Editor Howell Talley" painted on the glass door. I saw Mrs. Hoffman enter and talk to him. Talley's face winced slightly with a vexed expression, and I saw him glance at me. Then he came out and gestured for me to come into the office. As I entered he said, "Mary tells me you want to be a reporter."

"Yes, sir," I said.

Talley gestured for me to sit down then took his own chair behind the desk. He asked about my experience. I had none, I said, but I could do it if given a chance.

"Well," he said, the word long and drawn out. "It turns out we do have an opening here. But I'm not sure you're the one to fill it. We had a reporter just up and quit Friday without notice. He just said he was leaving."

What incredible luck, I thought. A guy quits on Friday and I show up the following Monday. Confederate Memorial Day, no less.

We talked a while longer, and he winced with compassion when I told him we had four children. Then I thumbed a ride back to Wellington, grabbed up the two stories I had published, and caught another ride back to Gadsden. Talley said he would read the stories and be back in touch. I gave him the Sharptons' phone number.

On Wednesday, April 29, I was outside throwing rocks at trees. In the early afternoon, after my third TD pass with the rocks, Louise came to the front porch and shouted, "Frank, you got a phone call."

I ran to the house. It was Talley. "Frank," he said, "we're going to give you a chance at this job. Can you be at work at about eight-thirty in the morning?"

"I can be there at six o'clock," I said.

"There's no need to get here *that* early," he said. "But I need to tell you there will be a two-week probation period. If you don't work out, you'll leave."

"I'll do my best," I said.

10

For the first several days I was given training in newspaper basics: how to edit stories, how to write heads, the different sizes of type, and so on. I was given a desk with a Royal typewriter. The staff was small. There were only eleven people in the entire editorial department, including sports and society news.

After several days of basic instruction, I was given the chance to write a story. Talley told me, "Go out and see what you can find to write about. Then do it. This is your chance to see what you can do."

I had read an Associated Press calendar of events and recalled that May 8 was the anniversary of the end of World War Two in Europe—VE Day. By sheer luck I went by the Army recruiting office, and one of the men, Sgt. Hoyt Greene, had been in Germany when the war ended. I talked to him for an hour or so. He told me how he had felt that day in 1945: "It was like a flower opening. The war was over and I was alive."

What better way to start a story? I was surprised and excited when the paper came out the next day with my story on the top two left columns of the front page.

My first regular assignment was to be editor of a section called "News Parade." It was the one-fourth page given to news of black people. It ran twice a week.

The writer was a black schoolteacher named Harriet Waller. She wrote about births, deaths, weddings, church events, and so on. My job was to trim her material down so it fit within the allotted space.

The first day I was to meet her brought a quandary: here I was in the South, where race was a major concern at every level. I was an outsider, new on the job. When Mrs. Waller came in, was I to stand and greet her as I had been taught? Or should I just sit there at my desk? I honestly didn't know. I didn't want to offend anyone, and I didn't want to hurt my chances at keeping the job.

So that afternoon she came in, a neatly dressed woman with a charming smile. I stood up immediately and held out my hand.

No one in the newsroom showed the slightest surprise, as I might have expected. In fact, Arthur Shaw, the young city editor, also stood and walked over to greet her and to make a formal introduction.

When he had returned to his desk, Mrs. Waller turned to me and said, "Oh, I want you to know we are proud to have this space each week. You know, we worked hard to get it. But I hope in time you will be able to help us get a little more. There's so much news out there, and we can't always get everything in."

"Well, I'll do my best," I said.

She handed me the folder that contained her stories. "These are for Sunday," she said. "I know it's more than usual, but maybe you can find a way to get them into the paper."

I did, but to do it meant cutting many of the short stories to even shorter items. There was no room to negotiate space, I was told. When Mrs. Waller came in the following Wednesday, she seemed a little humbled.

It was easy to understand why. I stood. "I'm sorry we had to trim some of the stories. I had to do it in order to get them in."

She nodded. "I was hoping the item about the wedding could have been kept intact. The newlyweds come from two of our most respected families."

I nodded. What could I say? One day a few months later, Mrs. Waller came in as usual and opened the file folder, taking one last look at her material. Then she handed it to me. "There's an item in there about one of our older residents. We're having a birthday party for her Sunday. I hope it can get in that day."

"How old is she going to be?" I asked.

"You might not believe it, but she is 110."

"She's that old?" I was amazed. "That means she was born in 1854."

Mrs. Waller smiled at my reaction. "That's right. She was born in slavery. She was seven when the Civil War started. She lived through that and through Reconstruction."

"That's a lot of history," I said.

"Do you think we could get a separate feature story on her?" she asked, gazing evenly at me. It was worth a full-blown story, and she knew it. So did I, as green as I was in the business. "We would appreciate anything you can do," she added.

When I relayed the idea, a sympathetic Talley shook his head. "I agree it's a great story, but we have just so much space and everything has to fit in there. Do what you can, but keep it within the space limits." We were being held within the constraints that someone had designed years before. We couldn't move too fast . . . not even with a good story.

Although the story ran longer than the other items in Mrs. Waller's column, it was still far too small when it was published. I found it hard to look her in the eye when she came that next Wednesday. However, the following week she hurried into the newsroom, her face glowing with excitement.

"Oh, did you see what happened to our story?" she asked.

I shrugged. "Something happened?"

"Yes, yes, it did," she said. "The *Atlanta Constitution* saw the item and ran a story about the birthday party and the fact that she had lived through slavery, the Civil War, and Reconstruction."

It was good news. But I reminded her that it was not our story; it was hers.

11

Not long before I got the job, Millie and I rented a house that had a well and running water for the kitchen sink. Pop Pearson, who was in his seventies, let us have it for $15 a month. There was an outhouse and space for a sizable garden. Most of the cooking was done in an electric frying pan. Millie even tried to make biscuits in there.

The house was a frame structure, very much like the one in which the Helmses lived. It had running water for the kitchen sink, but, given that I had come from a middle-income family, it still made for what I considered a spartan existence. My family's home in Byesville, Ohio, sat on a tree-lined street and had two living rooms, one containing a beautiful baby grand piano. There were two thousand people in my hometown, all of them white. And since my father owned a grocery story, we ate well. When we visited my parents in early March 1964, I thought of staying there until I found a job. But four little children running around changed that. My mother handed me two $20 bills and tearfully told me, "Dad thinks it best you go back to Alabama." My parents were gentle but firm in their insistence.

Our new place was about a quarter mile from where Robert and Louise lived. Quite often we would eat supper with them, and most of the time we had Sunday dinner there. Millie tried to cook, but she couldn't come close to equaling Louise, especially when it came to biscuits.

One Sunday after dinner, Robert, Mr. Helms, and I stood outside in the front yard. Robert owned a number of dogs, and the biggest and toughest of them was Rounder. He was king of the animals at the Sharpton home. But he became an absolute coward whenever a certain dog from up the road came by.

We called that beast "Bad Red" because of his color and his temperament. He just looked mean and vicious. A number of times I had observed him trotting boldly down the blacktop road, pausing from time to time to glower at Rounder. Nothing ever happened, though, because Rounder would lower his tail and slink to the ditch. If Bad Red came closer, Rounder would retreat to the yard and even to the back of the house, whimpering.

So on this Sunday there came Bad Red down the road. Rounder spotted him and meekly retired to the ditch, his tail down, his ears, and his pride, drooping.

Robert shook his head. "I don't know why in the devil Rounder is scared of that dog. He's bigger than him."

Mr. Helms nodded. "If he'd just stand up once, he could whup him."

We stood and watched as the red dog drew nearer. Rounder began to whine and back toward the three of us.

"Stand still there," Robert muttered. "Don't you be scared of that there dog."

Red stopped and fixed his meanest gaze on Rounder. But Rounder, perhaps fearing the humiliation of retreat in front of his owner, stood his ground in the ditch.

And then the red dog growled menacingly. He took one step, then two, toward Rounder. But Rounder didn't move. Then the red terror charged toward the ditch. Rounder yelped and rolled on his back. His assailant was on him, teeth bared.

There was a flurry of thrashing about, growling and whimpering and blood-chilling yelps of desperation. Above it all came Rounder's plaintive squeal, as if begging for mercy, his big rump swinging back and forth as he struggled to get free.

"Rounder!" Robert snapped. "Get up!"

In the ditch I noted Red flinch for a split second, attack again, then back off. Rounder was not only holding his own, he was forcing his attacker off of him. A change came over him, a realization that he was as strong—maybe stronger—than his opponent. Then in a flash Rounder rolled to his feet. There was a loud snap as teeth clacked. Again there was a loud whimpering sound . . . but this time it came from Bad Red. Now he was down on his back in the road, eyes wide with surprise and horror. Rounder pounced on top of him, his jaws locked on the intruder's neck.

Now it was Red who was yelping in terror. He was down and caught in a death clutch. Rounder's triumphant "GRRRR" rose over the road.

"Rounder!" Robert called sharply. "Let go! That's enough!"

Rounder obeyed, and Bad Red leaped to his feet and scurried down the road, tail down, casting furtive glances behind him. The whites of his eyes looked as big as hard-boiled eggs.

"Way to go, Rounder!" I called.

Robert and Mr. Helms were chuckling with pride. And Rounder, chest out and tail up, pranced along the road, darting once more toward Bad Red to hasten his departure. It was a resounding victory. The red dog would never again pass the house without first going to the ditch on the other side of the road. And he would always be in a hurry to get by.

"Funny about dogs," said Mr. Helms. "Sometimes the big ones let the little ones get the best of 'em."

"That's right," Robert agreed.

And Mr. Helms continued. "If a little dog knows what to do, he can sure-enough whup a bigger one."

I was sure there would be a story to follow. And there was.

He spit tobacco juice, paused a moment, eyes twinkling, then nodded down toward the crossroads, where the tracks crossed near the Post Office as well as Yaikow's store.

"I saw this big dog come along the road down there once," Mr. Helms said. "Acted like he was the top thing in the world. So as he was goin' along, here comes this little dog, one of those furry little ones. Well, that big dog growls at him and barks, tryin' to scare him, I reckon. Well, the little dog stepped back. Then, as the big one went prancin' by, the little one comes up from behind and he gets ahold of the big one's balls. Clamps his teeth down on 'em. Well, you never heard such a racket."

Robert and I were laughing now, and Mr. Helms had to struggle to keep his voice firm.

But he went on: "The big dog takes off down the road toward the tracks and the little one is right there, just hangin' on with his teeth, almost flyin' along in the air. He just wouldn't let go. And all the while the big dog is squealin' like he was fixin' to die."

"I'll bet he wished he was dead," Robert muttered, grinning.

Mr. Helms nodded. "Well, the little one hung on for about as far as from here to that house out yunder, then he finally let go."

"What happened to the big dog?" I asked.

"Well, we never seen hide nor hair of him after that." Mr. Helms stared down the road toward the track intersection. "I'll bet you one thing. He was sorry he ever showed up here in the first place."

12

Dan and Minnie Belle Helms came from different parts of the South, but both shared similar roots. She was born in Mississippi and had Indian blood in her lineage, probably Choctaw. Mr. Helms grew up in the northeastern part of Alabama, near Fort Payne. He, too, was part Indian, most likely Cherokee.

They were married after World War I. He served in the Army and remembered being at Camp McClellan, near Anniston. He didn't have to go overseas, but he was faced with the prospect of death nonetheless—the 1918 scourge of the Spanish flu. The disease killed thousands across the land. About five thousand died in Alabama alone. He recalled seeing the coffins stacked up at the Army post, as soldiers collapsed and died. It was such a severe outbreak that Birmingham residents wore surgical masks to and from work or shopping. On one Sunday churches canceled services; the *Birmingham News* published a prayer for those who held their worship at home.

But in the years following their marriage they were often drawn to family gatherings in the Fort Payne area. The town sits in a valley between Sand Mountain and Lookout Mountain. These gatherings included the traditional family reunions and the Decoration Day ceremonies at old graveyards where ancestors were buried.

The latter events, held in the spring, included dinner on the grounds. Tables were set up under shade trees that fringed the cemetery, and dozens of bowls were set out, filled with cornbread, biscuits, fried chicken, baked beans, and apple and peach pies. Big jars were filled with tea or Kool-Aid.

Louise told me about the point of it all. "It's sharing a meal with them that's gone ahead of us," she said. "We're here alive, but we believe they are here with us in spirit. It's like a celebration."

Along with the food and a service, families brought flowers to decorate the graves. Some of the markers dated well back into the early 1800s. Some were Civil War veterans; others had been in World War I, World War II, and Korea. And many were infants who had died of the flu. At one place in the cemetery no less than five children were buried, their headstones indicating they had died before reaching their seventh birthday.

"Gone home to Jesus," some of the faded markers read.

Sad stories, I thought. They contrasted with the lively chatter and sumptuous feast being enjoyed. When the meal ended, a trio—a woman and two men—strummed guitars and sang some of the old favorites, such as "Shall We Gather by the River" and "I'll Fly Away."

As the singing continued, the people nodded slowly, and some approved by "um-hmm"; some wept silently. This event made me feel closer to the Helms family and to the traditions of the southern people. These were hill folks, the ones who enjoyed the "Grand Ole Opry" and who arose early to hear the farm reports on the radio. In the afternoons they looked at magazines such as the *Progressive Farmer* or *Home Life.* They were touched by simple things and appreciated moments of sympathy. Most of them listened to WVOK in Birmingham, to a man named Joe Rumore, who spoke in a friendly, person-to-person manner. Once, when tornadoes had ravaged the state the night before, he opened his broadcast without saying anything. He simply began by playing "Amazing Grace," the version recorded by Judy Collins. That type of beginning was in the same spirit as Decoration Day.

Once we went to a family reunion near Fort Payne. It was a summer day, but the big oaks that towered over the rambling country home provided shade; a breeze kept things comfortable. Along with chicken and baked beans, there was one long table that was loaded with watermelons and at least twenty cakes and pies.

After eating, the people sat on the porch and at the benches and watched the sunbeams dapple their way through the oaks. They talked about the "dear departed," the chances for rain, and how the gardens were doing.

It was at this mellow moment that Millie and Mr. Helms told me about Pete Wooten, a man who was in his sixties, a man who was a member of this family.

"Who is Pete Wooten?" I asked.

"Maybe you'll see him," Millie responded. "He might show up here. This is his family. He's a cousin to me."

There was a tinge of mystery to the way she said it. I waited to hear more.

"The law is still lookin' for him," said Mr. Helms.

"The law?" I was suddenly interested. "What'd he do?"

"Pete killed his son-in-law," Mr. Helms said, taking a quick glance at the surrounding hills. "So they think he might show up here. But he might not. It's been a while."

Millie told me that the son-in-law had mistreated his wife, who was Pete's daughter. Pete had tolerated some of it for a time but finally had had enough. He got his shotgun and gunned the man down. It was a plain case of southern justice, most of the family felt. It had happened years before, and Pete had taken off, vanishing into the woods that covered great stretches of Lookout Mountain. No one had seen him since . . . or rather, no one in the family had admitted to the sheriff that they had seen him. When this information was given, Mr. Helms grinned wryly and gave me a wink.

But after hearing the story, it seemed to me that a number of the family members—and there must have been fifty of them there—kept glancing toward the woods from time to time. I suspected some thought that old Pete might finally return home. What better time than at a family reunion?

13

At times the pace of living in Wellington was snail-like. No one hurried. The nearest thing to a scheduled event was Mr. Helms's slow walk to the U.S. Post Office each morning around eleven o'clock. Sometimes he might leave a little early and stop off at Yaikow's store to get a tin of Copenhagen snuff. About the only telephone calls that came to the Helms house were from Louise; or sometimes Aunt Rose, who was nearly ninety, might call. She was Mrs. Helms's older sister.

Yaikow's store should have been in one of Norman Rockwell's paintings. It was a part of what defined the South in the 1950s and 1960s. In fact, it looked like it would be at home in a picture of the early 1930s. The store was actually a house with brown tarpaper on the exterior. There was a front porch with a bench on it and a Royal Crown Cola sign above the overhang. Smaller signs advertising Lucky Strike cigarettes and Red Man chewing tobacco were on the facing by the door. There was even a smaller sign on the screen door. Inside, the living room had been converted into the business enterprise. Mrs. Yaikow stood behind the counter, which contained jars of jawbreakers and cinnamon sticks. Behind her on the wall was the cigarette rack. Above it was a picture of a brown-skinned girl proclaiming the great taste of Fatima cigarettes. There was a bread rack with some pastries, a small freezer with ice cream and Popsicles, and a refrigerator for milk.

Most customers bought things on credit and paid at the first of each month when their Social Security checks came in. The store captured the slow pace of life in Wellington at the time.

It was a good place to visit on a hot summer day. In winter a coal stove provided warmth. The Yaikows lived in the back part of the structure.

Mrs. Yaikow usually waited on customers, and she said little, just waited until you picked out what you wanted. Then she'd say something like, "Will that do it?" When you said that was it, she would tell you how much you owed. Then she would either take the money or write down the amount on a charge ticket.

One day we were at Louise's house for lunch, which everybody there called dinner. Mr. and Mrs. Helms had come up to join us. Afterward we went to the living room. The spring day was sunny and mild, and earlier Millie had commented on how serene her mother seemed to be.

There had been a discussion about Mr. Helms going to Yaikow's to pick up an extra tin of snuff. He responded by saying it could wait until they were going back home.

To my surprise, she agreed it would make good sense to wait.

As we relaxed in the living room, Mr. Helms told us about his visit to Yaikow's the previous afternoon. The talk, he said, was about a neighbor down the road having a problem with his mule.

At that moment we heard someone walk onto the porch. Then the screen door opened and a tall, graying man entered the room.

Mr. Helms looked up and nodded at the fellow, and the visitor nodded back, saying, "How y'all doin' today?"

"Well, reckon we're just about right," Mr. Helms replied. "How about you?"

"Oh, fair, I reckon," the man said. He was wearing a pair of bib overalls, with the straps over the shoulders. The pocket of his white, long-sleeve shirt bulged with what appeared to be a can of snuff.

Mrs. Helms nodded slowly, then muttered, "Yeah, we're a-doin' about as well as you might expect for old folks."

With that, they all nodded.

The man kept standing there and finally Louise offered, "Have you a seat there, if you can find a place."

The old fellow then sat down on a foot stand that was near the television set. For a time no one said anything. I was sipping a cup of coffee, saying nothing, just watching. Millie and Louise sat on the couch beside Mrs. Helms, who was staring vacantly at the floor.

Finally, Mr. Helms remarked, "I was talkin' to a man the other day at the store and he was tellin' me he was tryin' to have his garden plowed up, but he said the mule has been actin' more contrary than usual. Couldn't get it to move nary an inch."

There was a long pause while the visitor pondered over the situation. Then: "Why, I swaney," he declared softly. "That mule's hidebound. I've heard of such."

Mr. Helms nodded. "Some of 'em can get that way."

"Hidebound?" I asked. "Is that what you said?"

The visitor peered at me a moment, probably reacting to the northern accent. Then he said, "Yeah, they say a mule's skin can get so tight he can't move. Call it 'hidebound.' Leastways that's what I've always heard."

There was a long silence. Well, now I'd heard about everything.

Finally the visitor arose and said, "Well, I best be goin'. Been down towards Alexandria visitin' some of the folks there."

"Hmmm," Mr. Helms grunted, nodding.

"They all doin' fine," the man advised, as though we were interested. Then, he opened the door, paused, and said, "Y'all come go with me."

"Just stay with us," was Mr. Helms's low-key response.

Then the man left. There was another long silence. Mrs. Helms kept staring at the floor, a hand on her chin. Finally, as though musing aloud, she asked, "Dan, who was that man?"

He turned his head slowly toward her. "I ain't never laid eyes on him before," he said, matter-of-factly. "Thought he was some kin of yours."

She shook her head. With a puzzled smile, she opined, "I got no idee who he was."

"Well, Momma," Louise said with a surprised smile, "I thought both of you knew who he was, the way he just walked in here."

"Me too," said Millie. "I thought all of you knew him."

I marveled at the innocent hospitality. Then they pondered about it for fifteen or twenty minutes. And then the incident was concluded when Mrs. Helms intoned a long, "Well-ll . . . "

We never did find out who the man was. Apparently he came to the wrong house.

14

You know how you sometimes think a house might be haunted? Well, I never had that feeling about the Helms house. Not until the day that Mr. Helms told a story about the place, something that happened before he and Minnie Belle moved in.

It was a rainy night and the TV reception was not good. Anyway, Mr. Helms, seated in his rocking chair, and with a fresh dip of snuff in his mouth, began the account.

"Once, there was a good soakin' rain like this," he said. "And the people that lived here had a garden out back. I guess the corn was yea high"—and he raised his arms to about shoulder height. "Well, one night after they had gone to bed and been asleep a while, they got woke up when he hears this cow bellowin' out in the back. The man gets up and says that there was a cow in the corn patch, and it was liable to knock over some of it. But he couldn't see anything. Just kept hearin' that cow bellow. Figured it had got out of somebody's pasture. Next mornin' he goes out and looks at the patch, and some of the corn has been eaten and knocked down. So as wet as it was, he went out into the patch and looked for tracks. Thought he might be able to trail the thing back from where it had come. But when he gets out there lookin' at it, there ain't the first cow track. All he can find is a man's footprints, and they're barefoot. Wasn't the first cow print there."

There was a long pause then, and Millie and I exchanged glances. Finally she said, "There are a lot of strange things that have gone on around here."

I shook my head, "A barefoot man who bellows like a cow? What could be stranger?"

"If it was a man," Mr. Helms muttered, letting the words hang over the room. Nobody spoke. There was only the sound of the rain spattering on the roof. Of course there were always the stories that the devil took the form of a cow. Or a goat, I wasn't sure.

"Is that a true story?" I asked. I had to be a little skeptical.

Mr. Helms nodded, gazing at the floor. "They say it's true."

"Tell him about the jackman's lantern, Daddy," Millie said.

"The what?" I hadn't heard that term before.

"Jackman's lantern is what they call it," Millie said. "Tell him."

Mr. Helms rocked a few times. Then: "We lived down by Coldwater Creek. I guess it's fifteen miles or so from here. I worked at a pipe shop in Anniston. Got off about eleven o'clock each night. Walked home. One night I was walkin' home, and it was through a patch of woods. As I was goin' along I happened to look off into the woods 'cause I saw something movin' there. Well, I saw this orange ball, and it was just floating along in the woods, dead even with me."

At that point I felt a distinct chill in the room. I leaned forward to listen more closely.

He went on: "So I started walkin' faster, 'cause I didn't know what it was. It wasn't a man with a lantern or anything, 'cause there was no sound. It just kept floating there. I started runnin' then. Glanced over into the woods and the thing was right there. I couldn't get away from it."

"What happened?" I asked.

"Well, I finally reached the house and the woods ended just before I got there. I ran up to the front porch and looked over yunder and it was just hangin' there on the edge of the woods, like it was watchin' me," he said. "It didn't come no further. I went in the house and didn't look out the windows that night."

A long pause then. Mr. Helms eased back into the rocker and shook his head, showing that even after all those years, he was still mystified.

"Well, what do you think it was?" I asked.

"Don't know," he said. "There's been stories about jackman's lanterns seen around here for a long time."

Another silence. Then Mrs. Helms muttered, "Lots of strange things. Some say the lanterns are dead people come back to look for . . . I don't know what. I guess lookin' for whatever it is that ghosts look for."

Well, so much malarkey, I thought to myself. But aloud, I said, "All regions have their folklore." Then realizing that I might have affronted Mr. Helms and his story, I hastily injected: "But that's not to say that some of them aren't true. I'm sure you saw what you saw that night."

But I kept thinking about the cow story . . . or whatever it was. A few nights later, after everyone had gone to bed, I realized that I had to go to the outhouse. That meant passing the back corn patch down the narrow walkway, which consisted of foot-wide planks.

A visit to the outhouse at night is nothing to be nostalgic about. I got a flashlight, then woke up Millie to tell her I was going out, grabbed Mr. Helms's twelve-gauge shotgun and eased out the back door, which creaked loudly as it shut.

A quarter moon was out, and drapes of mist hung from the black gum tree in the back part of the old homesite. In case anyone or anything was hiding, I called out loudly, "This old twelve gauge kicks like a mule when it goes off. Hope I don't have to use it."

To my reassurance, there was no answer. Even the dogs were quiet.

Have you ever been to an outhouse at night? It's an experience. Your imagination plays tricks on you. Are there spiders lurking by? Is that a snake in the corner there? You don't waste time.

And then I heard the distant bellowing of a cow that was prowling the pastures in the middle of the night. I took the footpath in record time, latched the backdoor and hurried to the front bedroom. Millie sat up.

"You take that shotgun with you?" she asked.

"Yeah. I took it with me," I said defensively. "Why?"

"It wouldn't have done any good," she said, then turned over and went back to sleep.

15

The shotgun dated back to the 1920s. Often Mr. Helms had gone hunting and brought home supper in the form of a wild turkey, a duck, or rabbits. But as he aged, he hunted less. The old gun, which just held one shell at a time, was propped up in the corner of the front bedroom for home defense. Not that the Helmses had much concern about intruders. They went to bed in the summer with the windows open, and mostly left the doors unlocked winter and summer.

One day I asked him about his shooting ability. He peered at me closely, then reached out and punched me lightly on the arm.

"I can hit what I shoot at," he said. "I learned to shoot before I ever went into the Army."

Then he told me about a time that the gun had saved his life. It had happened in the 1930s when he was hunting atop Lookout Mountain, north of Gadsden.

"I had a couple of dogs with me," he began. "It was in the fall, and leaves were starting to come down. Anyway, I was off up there by myself and the dogs had gone out ahead, yelpin' and makin' a racket, tryin' to flush out some quail or ducks or whatnot. Durn things got so far ahead of me I quit hearin' 'em anymore. Well, a little while later I hear 'em a-comin' back towards me. They was a-yelpin' and their ears was laid back like they was scared. Ran right by me. I was tryin' to figure out what scared 'em. About that time I heard the ground rumblin' and there comes a pack of wild pigs, headin' straight towards me. Them dogs led 'em right to me. Well, if they'd got ahold of me, they'd have killed me."

"Wild pigs," I said. "You always think of Porky Pig, fat and harmless."

He nodded. "Meanest things in the world. They'd rip you apart in a minute. So I hurried and climbed a little old tree, not real little, but not real big either. I got up there and waited and them pigs circled the tree and waited, gruntin' and snortin, waitin' on me."

"What'd you do?"

"Well, I sat there for a time, then I got the gun and aimed at one on the edge, farthest away from me," he went on. "I shot him. Killed him dead. Soon as he went down the others ran over there and started eatin' him right then. They was fightin' one another for the dead one. So I shot another one. Then another and another. Killed about seven or eight of 'em and the others just tore into them."

"Must have been scary," I said.

"It was a sight," he said, with a shake of his head. "Well, after about an hour, they got their fill and some of 'em started off. Then the rest of 'em followed after 'em. I waited a good long while, then came down and ran down the mountain till I saw a farmhouse and went there and told the old feller there about the pigs. So he got his rifle and got his wagon and team out of the barn and gave me a ride back to where I lived."

"So that gun saved your life," I said.

"Sure did. Shootin' that close I couldn't miss," he allowed, taking another dip of snuff. "But I'll tell you one thing: them pigs kept me from gettin' anything else that day. I come home and we didn't have nothin' but bread to eat."

Later that day I told Millie about the wild-pig story, and she laughed, saying she had heard it before. Then I remembered her remark about the gun not doing me any good if I needed it.

"Why'd you tell me that?" I asked.

"Because it wouldn't," she said.

I waited patiently for more details. Finally, she said, "Back when I was getting ready to graduate from high school Mother and Daddy got into a big argument. I don't remember what it was about, but she was mad like she always gets, and Daddy got mad, too. It was the first time I ever saw him get really mad. So she said something and he said he could kill her as quick as he could look at her."

It seemed out of character for Mr. Helms to show that much anger. "Really, your dad said that?"

"Yeah, he said it," she replied. "And you know what Mother did? She laughed at him and said he didn't have the guts to shoot her. Well, I had got the shotgun and took the firing pin out." Actually, she explained, Robert had helped her a few days before to get the pin loose because her parents had been in a serious argument and she feared things might get worse.

"What happened? Did your dad get the gun?"

"Yes, he did," Millie said. "He came in and put a shell in there and went back into the kitchen and held it. I went out there and tried to talk to them, tried to get them to stop. But Mother just laughed at him and even dared him to shoot her. Daddy held the gun up and pointed it right at her. She just kept laughing and daring him. But Daddy seemed to listen to me then, and he put the gun down, took the shell out and threw it across the room. He never pulled the trigger."

I shook my head. "Then he didn't know it wouldn't have fired."

"He never found out," Millie said, smiling.

"Well, what happened to the firing pin?" I asked.

"I lost it," she said. "Daddy never again picked the gun up, because by that time he had quit hunting."

I glanced at the shotgun standing in the corner. "So, if somebody breaks in here some night, that gun wouldn't do any good."

Millie shrugged. "It might. If you picked it up and pointed it at somebody, they'd never know it didn't have a firing pin."

One thing about Minnie Belle: as cantankerous as she was, you had to admit she had courage. Or maybe a death wish, I didn't know. Or maybe, I thought much later, she somehow knew the gun would not fire.

16

In June 1964, not long after I was hired by the *Gadsden Times,* we left Pop Pearson's house in Wellington and moved to Glencoe, a town seven miles nearer to the city. It had indoor plumbing, storm windows, and hardwood floors. The price was much higher, too. Pearson had charged us $15 a month; the new place cost $60 a month. But I was making $80 a week, and it was well within range.

Glencoe wasn't so far that we could not visit the home folks, which we did often. We were also there almost every Sunday, usually in time for dinner at Louise's.

One day Mrs. Helms called Millie and said there was an urgent family matter that needed some attention. When I asked what was going on, Millie shrugged, saying she hadn't been given details. It meant something was afoot. I was off that Thursday, so we drove over. Millie was close-mouthed about what might be going on—if she knew.

When we arrived at the old house, she and Mrs. Helms retired to a bedroom to talk. Mr. Helms was out in the living room, seated in the rocker, looking more glum than usual. Finally, he let out a long sigh and muttered, "Lord, Lord."

"Something wrong?" I asked, my interest piqued by the unusual behavior and silence.

But he shook his head. Then: "It ain't nothin' good."

Silence then. We simply sat and said nothing, except to jump up every now and then to get the children back from the road. Finally I went on the front porch and stood. It was early enough in the season for some of the daffodils to be showing broad green shoots amidst the yellow-brown grass along the fence line of the adjoining property. Some of the wisteria and forsythia were also swelling.

At last Millie came out and stood beside me, arms folded, gazing at the children. Finally she spoke: "Mother's mad and upset because James has been dating a teenage girl over in Jacksonville."

I glanced at her. "A teenage girl? Why, he must be in his forties, isn't he?"

"Forty," she said. "He's been spending his money on her. Even bought her a gold necklace and a diamond ring."

God, I thought, as poor as this family was, no one could afford such luxuries. No wonder Mrs. Helms was upset.

"But what can your mom do about it?"

I should have known better than to ask.

"She wants to go over there and find the girl and get the stuff back," Millie said.

"What? How's she going to get there?" Then I waved a hand in futility. "Why certainly. *You're* going to take her there. You know, you could end up getting killed over stuff like this. You ought to stay out of it."

Just then the front door opened, and Mrs. Helms came out, her head shaking in short, convulsive moves. Her eyes blazed with anger. "I give him cigarette money and he spends his money on some tramp," she said, her voice quivering. "Come on, Mildred. Let's go."

I watched them leave, shaking my head. Then Mr. Helms came out of the house, looking disturbed and relieved at the same time: fearing trouble, while at the same time at ease with his wife out of the house for a little while.

"They ought not to be pokin' into other folks' business," he declared.

I agreed. But it was Minnie Helms's way to be involved directly in the lives of her family. She had led the way back in World War II when she went to get James out of the Army. And now she was going to keep his life straight by confronting a teenage hussy. At least that was her way of thinking.

Time passed slowly. Then, after nearly three hours, I saw the car making the turn by the tall pine tree that carried the reminder of the 1954 tornado.

They entered the house without speaking. I figured Mrs. Helms didn't think it was any of my business. Later Millie came out, and we prepared to leave.

"What happened?" I inquired, unable to suppress my curiosity.

"Well, it took us a while to find the house where the girl stayed," she said. "But we finally got there and the girl came to the door."

"Then what?" I prodded. Getting information was like pulling teeth.

"Mother asked her if she was dating James, and when she said she was, Mother told her she didn't want her around James anymore, and she was to give back the things he bought her."

"What'd she say?"

"Hardly nothing," Millie said, with a smile that showed she was still surprised. "She took the necklace and ring off right then and handed them to us."

"Your mom didn't yell at her or threaten her?"

"No. She just looked at her. That was enough."

I didn't know the girl, but in a way I felt sorry for her: confronted by two strangers who gave her orders about what she could do, then took her jewelry to boot. But it all must have turned out all right, for later I heard the girl married a younger man shortly after the encounter with my mother-in-law.

17

Mr. Helms never spoke much about his garden, but it was clear he enjoyed being able to plow the land and watch things grow. He wasn't much for flowers, but when it came to vegetables, his work produced food not only for him and his wife but for others as well.

He abided by folklore when it came to planting. "You never plant beans when there are beans in the bowel," he told me. He believed that if you did plant them within two days or so of eating beans, the plants would not bear well. He also planted corn on the day of the new moon and after the leaves of the oak trees were about the size of a squirrel's ear. (I had read that one somewhere in an Indian book long before.) Be that as it may, his corn and beans were both heavy producers.

He sometimes planted winter squash in between the corn rows. The corn was the old-fashioned white field variety, which he and Mrs. Helms preferred. Some of the stalks grew to a height of eight feet or more. The ears were thick and tasted more of starch than sugar.

One evening in August he picked a stack of roasting ears and shucked them in the backyard, then brought them in for cooking. Uncle Lee had stopped by.

Most of the corn was cut off the ear, fried till it was well done, then made into a gravy.

As we ate I asked why they never planted yellow sweet corn, which was a favorite of my family in Ohio.

Uncle Lee allowed a rare smile as he gently scoffed, "Why, shoot, that's Yankee corn. It ain't fit to eat. This white corn is real corn."

It was hard to understand why they were reluctant to try some of the newer, more tasty varieties that had been developed. One could only speculate that the reason was the Civil War. There was such a lingering resentment against anything from the North that they would not lower themselves to try a corn developed at some university above the Mason-Dixon line. And second, it underscored the notion that these folks did not want *anything* to change, including their taste for corn.

I later talked to another man about the matter, and when I mentioned sweet corn, he shook his head and sneered, "Yankee corn. Why, I wouldn't feed it to my hogs."

But, regardless of his methods and beliefs, Dan Helms was a good gardener, and he spent many hours weeding and hoeing, a tireless worker even in his seventies.

On that first visit in August 1959 we took a tour of the garden, and out at the back part of the corn patch I saw a large green, warty squash growing; farther down was a huge watermelon.

We walked to look them over, and something caught my eye. Closer inspection revealed a gaping hole at the end of the squash. I pointed it out to Mr. Helms.

"Why, I'll be dogged," he said, bending lower. "Some critter took a big bite out of it. What in the world did that?"

The bite was about the size of a silver dollar, and it revealed the bright orange flesh of the squash. Whatever had bitten into it had backed away. Or else it ran when it heard us.

"Let me go look at the watermelon," he said, wiping the sweat off his face. As we walked, he called over his shoulder, "It ain't quite ripe . . . why, shoot! It done bit into this one, too."

I knelt beside it. One entire end of the melon was gone. I leaned closer to look inside.

"It not only took a bite; it's still in there eating," I said.

Mr. Helms frowned down at me. "What is it?"

"A turtle. He's just eating away."

"A turtle?" He shook his head. Then the look of disgust on his face turned to a faint smile. "Well, that beats all I ever seen. Reckon he likes watermelon better than squash."

"Want me to pull him out of there?"

Mr. Helms shook his head. "Naw, just leave him in there. It ain't gonna do us any good now. But I'm comin' back later and move him down the road. If I don't he'll eat my whole garden."

"That would have been a great watermelon," I said.

He nodded. Then, "This fella who lived up above Coates Bend grew him some big watermelons, I guess it must have been in the twenties or so. Anyway, he loaded them onto his wagon and rode up north a ways, up where men was cuttin' timber off Lookout Mountain. He stops where they're workin' and asks some of 'em on the road there if they want to buy a melon. Well, the men told him they didn't want any, but some of the workers up on the hillside would probably buy some."

Mr. Helms paused for a moment, collecting his thoughts. Then he went on: "So he gets down off the wagon and climbs up the side of Lookout Mountain, way up there, and tries to sell some melons. A few of the men said they'd like one, so he goes all the way back down to get one, which was about all he could carry at a time. But when he gets down the hillside to the wagon, the melons are all gone. The men who told him to go up the hill, they got all his melons. All he had was an empty wagon."

Then he chuckled about it. I nodded. It was a lesson. He lost his one melon to a turtle, but as the story clearly showed, it could have been much worse.

18

On June 22, 1964, I reported to work early at the *Gadsden Times.* There were a lot of stories about President Johnson preparing to sign a civil rights bill, and some of the newsroom talk was about the potential meaning of it all. While most of the people there were conservative and not overly keen on changing the social order, they were at the same time in support of blacks having certain rights.

It was sometime in the early afternoon that I heard Arthur Shaw saying, "That does not sound good at all." I went to see what he was talking about. A wire story came in announcing that the FBI said three civil rights workers were reported missing in a place called Philadelphia, Mississippi. By midweek the entire nation would know where Philadelphia, Mississippi, was located.

But another employee, who worked in another department, laughed about the wire story, saying, "Come on, Arthur. They probably just gone off somewhere having a good time."

That opinion was shared by a number of white southerners as the mystery continued to grow into a national story.

A few days later I talked with Mr. Helms about it. He was cutting some weeds near the edge of his garden. When I asked his opinion about the missing trio, he stopped working, wiped at his forehead, then shook his head.

"Don't rightly know," he said. "They could just be tellin' a story like that to get money from some of the rich people up North."

"You really think that?" I asked.

He started cutting the weeds again. For the next ten minutes or so I stood watching him. Finally, he stopped, and shook his head again.

"If you ask me, I think they dead somewheres over there," he said. "The Kluxers don't take folks off and tie 'em up somewhere. They either hang 'em or shoot 'em. They could be in one of them swamps or rivers over there and nary a soul will ever find 'em."

"It's sort of scary, isn't it," I said.

"Yep. The Kluxers can scare folks pretty bad," he said, "but if they was a-scarin' 'em this time, they'd have been back by now. I'm talkin' about over there in Mississippi. This don't seem like scarin'; this seems like they been killed, if you ask me."

"You ever been in the Klan?" I asked. I felt I could ask him and trust him to be truthful. Or maybe I should have minded my own business. But I asked.

"Naw. But I seen 'em ridin' around way back yunder, saw 'em a few times," he said. "They'd be on horses. I heard tell they went to one man's house—he was a white man—and they called him out and gave him a few good licks on the back with a whip. See, they said he hadn't been a-takin' good care of his family. They told him to go to work and behave. A while later, couple weeks, I reckon, they rode back and went into his kitchen. He had bacon, flour, coffee, all sorts of stuff for his family to eat. So they left. Didn't bother him no more."

"What about the Negro people?" I asked. "Any of them bothered by the Klan, I mean around here?"

"Way back yunder they sure enough did," he said, matter-of-factly. "I heard once where they got after this colored fella who had been doin' somethin' they didn't like. So one night they rode to his house and he was scared to come out, but some of his folks did. So they stood there and the leader told 'em he wanted a drink of water. Told 'em to bring him a bucket full of water. So they did and he raised the bucket up and drank it all. But what they didn't know was that he had a big bucket hid under his robe. They thought he drank the whole bucket. It scared 'em."

"So that was just to scare them, not to really hurt them?"

He nodded, then he said, "But they couldn't always scare the colored folks. One man down around Cleburne County somewhere, he didn't scare. The Kluxers came ridin' up one night and he came out on the front porch. Had him one of those repeatin' rifles. He saw them white robes they wore and he commenced shootin' fast as he could. They started fallin' off their horses. Killed four or five. Don't reckon the law ever did nothin' to him."

While Mr. Helms didn't disagree with some of the KKK tactics, he did not approve of such things as had happened in Philadelphia. The three young men—James Chaney, who was black, and Andrew Goodman and Michael Schwerner, who were white—were still missing on July 2 when President Johnson signed the Civil Rights Act of 1964.

It was just before noon on July 3, 1964, when Frank Helderman Jr., the general manager of the *Gadsden Times,* came to the newsroom and told me, "How about going up town and see what's going on, now that they've signed the civil rights bill."

I stood up with some hesitation. "Okay. But what am I looking for?"

"Well, just see what's going on, you know . . . see if there's any trouble or anything."

Actually, I didn't know what to expect. Were the black folks going to be dancing in the streets? Or running amok in Grant's Department Store? Or what?

So I got a notebook and walked the block to Broad Street. It was clear it was a special day. The sidewalks were thick with black people, some of them dressed in what appeared to be their Sunday best. One large woman in a red dress carried an umbrella and raised it up and down like a drum major. She was laughing loudly as she led a group of children toward Grant's. There was an air of revelry over the town. As I walked about, it seemed that most white people decided to stay at home. It was a strange sight in a way. I went into Grant's to look at the lunch counter. It was closed.

The signing of the bill meant black people could go into any public facility, such as a restaurant or motel, and could not be turned away because of their race. It was a piece of history that I was observing that day, but I was finding very little to write about.

I went back to the newspaper office. Helderman was still in the newsroom, waiting with a group of other workers. As I entered he called, "Anything going on?"

"Not much," I said. "A lot of people out shopping. A lot of Negro people are in town. That's about all."

"There's always a bunch of people shopping before a holiday," he noted.

Somebody, I don't remember who, remarked, "Maybe we'll get through all this with no trouble."

And we did. The day came and went peacefully.

I was still catching a ride home with Robert. I'd usually walk down to Meighan Boulevard and wait by a fruit and vegetable stand. I never said much to the man who worked there. He was about thirty or so, lean but muscular with dark-brown hair. He had tattoos on his arms. I suspected he might have spent some time in prison.

As I waited, he called to me: "Lots of niggers in town today." He was plainly agitated. "Old Johnson's going to let 'em take over the place. But not here."

And with that he reached behind the little counter and produced what appeared to be an oversized night stick, about the size of a baseball bat. He held it up for me to see it better.

"What's that for?" I didn't want to appear overly impressed.

He grinned and wagged it up and down. "Just in case I have to do some head-knockin'."

I told him everything seemed peaceful. But at that moment two young black men came into view on the other side of Meighan and started to cross. They seemed more interested in their conversation than in the fact that it was a historic day.

But the stand operator raised his club and glared at them. He took a few steps toward them. Alarmed, I backed away from him.

"What are you doing?" I asked.

"If they try to come here I'm gonna bust some heads," he growled. "Get ready."

I waved my arms at him. "Hold on there. They're not doing anything. You need to put that down."

Now he glared at me. "You want 'em to walk all over us?"

"They're not walking over anybody," I said. "They're just passing by."

Sure enough the two went up the street that led to Broad. They never gave us a glance. The man put the club down and walked away from me. We never spoke again, and I chose another place to meet Robert.

It was a day of transition, the beginning of something, as well as the ending of something. At day's end, however, it seemed like any other.

19

Gadsden had its share of racists, but it probably had no more than any other city or town in the South, or even the North. One Saturday night I went to police headquarters to see if there had been any arrests or anything else of interest. A sergeant leafed through some papers and shook his head.

"Nothing going on tonight," he said. Then with a brief chuckle, he added, "Unless you want to write about this nigger that was killed. But we don't even count them."

I asked him what happened. The sergeant replied that a man had become drunk and angry and threatened his wife. The woman's son, who was sixteen or so, picked up a baseball bat and struck the man over the head, killing him.

It was a terrible situation, I said.

"Yeah, but it solved the problem," said the sergeant.

On another occasion the county coroner, Noble Yocum, talked to me about racial problems and the disdain with which many officials viewed blacks. He showed me a death report filed by another coroner some years before. A black man had died in what appeared to be mysterious circumstances. In the "Cause of Death" space, the coroner had written, "Stopped breathing."

I was often confused by the race relations here. Blacks were viewed as secondary citizens, but at times there seemed to be some cordial relations when you least expected it.

We were at Robert's house one stormy night and had finished eating. We all were content to have the TV set off while we sat back and listened to the soothing rhythm of rainfall on the roof. The gas heater flickered blue-and-orange flames.

Suddenly, there was a knock at the door, the sound startling us.

"Well who in the world is a-comin' here on a night like this?" Mrs. Helms muttered.

I was sitting in the seat nearest the entrance. I looked at Robert. "Want me to answer it?"

He was squatted down in front of the gas heater. "Yeah, see who it is," he said.

I opened the door and a gust of cold wind blew in. The bulb on the front porch was blown, but in the darkness the figures of two black men could be seen standing there. Both looked drenched. The one in front took off his hat and asked, "Marse Robert be at home?"

I turned. "Robert, somebody wants to see you."

Robert stood and moved slowly to the door. Then he called out in a low voice, "Hey, Henry. John."

I heard one of them saying something. Robert puffed on his Camel, nodded several times. Then he said, "Okay. Let me get my coat and hat. Kinda wet out there. Y'all can step in if you like."

The two entered. The second one removed his hat. They nodded and repeated several times, "Evenin'. How y'all?

Standing in the kitchen door, Louise asked, "What is it?"

"Their car broke down and they need a ride," Robert muttered. "One of their relatives is real sick."

"We'll pay for the gas," one of the men said.

"Don't worry about the gas," Robert called. "It ain't that far."

As he got on his coat, I asked, "Want me to ride with you?"

"Naw," Robert said. "I have to carry them somewheres every once in a while. They'd do the same for me. I won't be gone long."

After he left, I looked at Millie. "I swear one of them called him 'Marse Robert.' Can you believe it?"

Louise shrugged. "That's what some of 'em call him. I've heard 'em call him that before. They're good people. They live up the road here. It's a bad night to be out, but they can't help it if their car breaks down. I swear, that's all cars are good for, seems to me. At least the ones we can afford."

"That's the way it goes with all of us in this family," Mrs. Helms said. "Wouldn't surprise me if Robert don't break down sometimes."

But in a half hour he returned.

20

If I didn't always understand race relations, it was at times more difficult to try to understand the breakdown of interfamily relations, which often were strained as a result of Mrs. Helms's sudden changes in mood.

Something as routine as going to wash clothes at a Laundromat in Jacksonville might explode into a furious argument. Sometimes Mr. Helms and I would ease out the back door to get away from it.

There had been several of these, and one could never pinpoint the cause. A typical breakdown started one morning shortly after Louise had sent her children off to school.

Mr. and Mrs. Helms had been brought to the house an hour earlier, their laundry sacked in a shopping bag. Louise had gone to pick them up.

"Well, I'm ready to go," Mrs. Helms had declared, almost immediately on entering the house.

But Louise wasn't. She still had to prepare breakfast for the kids, help them find books, find socks that were mates, sign a note the teacher had sent for one of them, do some yelling to get them out the door on time, then try to settle down and eat something herself and have some coffee. By then, she had a slight headache. It was enough to give anyone a headache.

At that moment, her voice slightly edged with impatience, Mrs. Helms had called out from the living room, "Louise, I'm ready to go. I've got to get back and do some things."

With a weary sigh and a glance at Millie, Louise replied, "Momma, I'm not ready yet. I still got to get my clothes together. And what do you have to do when you get back?"

"Things, Louise. I've got to feed the dogs and—"

"Daddy feeds the dogs, Momma," Louise interrupted.

Silence . . . a long, chill silence . . . so chill that it felt like the air might crack.

Then, in a conciliatory tone, Mr. Helms said, "We both feed 'em sometimes." He was aware of where this conversation was going. He was trying to stave it off.

I was in the kitchen with Millie and Louise. Then, from the living room, Mrs. Helms, in a low voice, muttered: "Hmmp. I got my things gathered up last night. If you're gonna wash, you ought to have your stuff ready. Can't sit around all day waitin'. Don't know why she can't get ready on time."

Well, that was the last straw as far as Louise was concerned. She got up from the table and stormed into the living room.

"Well, Momma, if all I had to do was get up and get clothes ready, I'd be ready, too!" she cried loudly. "But I have other things to do. I don't have just a few dogs to feed, neither. Now when I get ready, we'll go, so there's no need in you keeping on about it 'cause we ain't going before then."

There was a bristling silence. In the kitchen Millie and I exchanged glances and raised eyebrows. Louise could whip up a temper when she was pushed far enough.

The silence continued. We heard Mr. Helms clear his throat. Then, as expected, Mrs. Helms's shrill voice rang out:

"Well, the devil with y'all! I been sittin' here all mornin' waitin' to do just one load of clothes, but no! We can't do it. Why? Because you ain't ready. Louise can't get her things gathered up."

"Momma, I told you we'd go when I could get ready. And—"

"Well, durn!" called Mrs. Helms in a high-pitched voice. "If that's the way you're gonna be, then I just won't go. You can go by yourself." Then: "Come on, Dan. We'll just walk to the house."

Now Millie got into it, standing beside Louise. "Now Mother, don't be like that."

"Don't be like what?" Mrs. Helms fumed.

"You're acting like a child."

At the kitchen table I winced. That was the wrong thing to say.

"Come on, Dan!" Mrs. Helms thundered. "We're a-goin' home. We don't need not nary one of 'em. I'll wash the durn things out by hand if it takes all night."

And with that she went out the door. Mr. Helms trailed behind, carrying the bag of laundry, staggering slightly as he went down the steps.

Louise retired to the bedroom. The headache had worsened, I was sure. Millie waited a moment or two, then got my keys. "I'll go take Mother and Daddy home."

I watched from the porch. Millie pulled up beside them and stopped, but they wouldn't get in. Mr. Helms started to, but Mrs. Helms kept walking. Finally, she stopped and there was some talk. Then she got into the car, and Mr. Helms followed. Millie drove them to their house, which was about a half mile away, and, minutes later, was back.

We sat in the living room for an hour or so. Then Louise emerged, told us she was sorry we had to hear such an argument, and began getting the laundry together.

"You just can't say a thing to Momma," she said. "She just goes off the handle, and nothing you say can change it."

"I know," said Millie. "She's always been that way."

About an hour later—it was now close to 10:30—we drove down to the Helms's house. Mr. Helms was in the living room. Mrs. Helms was in bed with a headache. Louise and Millie went in to talk to her. There was no more arguing. But when they emerged, Mrs. Helms had been crying, and Louise was wiping tears from her eyes. I assumed peace had been restored.

"Well, Momma, if you're ready, I guess we can go," Louise said in a contrite tone.

"I'm ready, I reckon," her mother replied.

Good grief, I thought to myself, if she had said, "I've been ready since seven this mornin'," the whole thing could have started again.

21

In August 1964 the FBI found the bodies of the three civil rights workers in Mississippi. They had been buried in an earthen dam on a farm. All had been shot. At the time there were no arrests, although the FBI had questioned the sheriff of Neshoba County, Lawrence Rainey, and his chief deputy, Cecil Price.

When we talked about it later, Mr. and Mrs. Helms were in agreement that it had been a terrible thing and that somebody should pay.

"It seems to me they'd have been better off stayin' up North where they belonged," Mrs. Helms opined. "They shouldn't have been down here stirrin' up the colored people."

Millie said, "They were there trying to get the Negro people interested in trying to vote."

Mrs. Helms threw a hand up listlessly and shook her head. "I don't care what it was they was a-doin'; they should have stayed up where they belonged."

"There's plenty of colored folks up North that need help," Mr. Helms suggested, glancing at me and nodding his head several times for emphasis. "Ain't that right?"

Well, I had to agree with that. But I added, "They had a right to be in Mississippi. It's a part of the U.S."

"You ain't got no right to cause trouble, or stir folks up so there is trouble," Mrs. Helms shot back. "If they'd stayed at home where they belonged, they'd be a-livin' right now. That's all I got to say about it."

"Well, I'm sure they'd still be living if they'd stayed at home," I agreed.

Millie, who was quite a ways along in her fifth pregnancy, gave me a warning nod to avoid a conflict, and I changed the subject to the weather.

The weather was indeed a topic. Because of the dry spell the water level in the well was too low to be used. We had come to help Mr. and Mrs. Helms get some water at a spring that was not far away.

Louise drove up about that time, her green station wagon loaded with empty plastic jugs and some glass jars. We put some plastic jugs in the back of my car and started out.

While the Helmses had the well on the back porch, Louise usually relied on getting spring water. She kept a barrel under the overhang of the roof and caught enough rainwater to wash dishes and to give the dogs. But for drinking and cooking, she made the drive to the spring about once a week.

Angel Springs was a gurgling oasis nestled in a grove of low-hanging willows, oak saplings, and a tree that I think was a honey locust. The spring was the start of a small stream that weaved through the nearby meadow. It faded away into a stand of taller hardwood and pine.

As we pulled into the small, dusty trail that led to the spring, we observed a red pickup truck parked nearby. I saw several black people toting jugs to and from the water.

Getting out of the car, Mr. Helms called to me from the station wagon, "Hold on a bit. Let them get their water first. Then we'll go down."

We waited, and when the others had finished, we began to unload our jugs and jars.

There were two black women and one man. As they got into their pickup truck, the man nodded and called out, "Evenin'."

Mr. Helms called back, "Evenin'."

Then we went to the spring. I took off my shoes and waded into the cold, ankle-deep water, staying downstream from the outflow.

With the trees above and the brisk water, it was a cool place to be on a hot August day.

I cupped my hands and drank from the spring. "Great taste."

"Best water you can find around these parts," Mr. Helms said. "Makes good coffee."

We finished filling the containers and were loading them in the car when we heard the low but distinct rumble of thunder.

"Might get some rain now," said Mrs. Helms.

We glanced up at the sky, which showed a few strands of graying clouds.

"Might be enough to fill that well up some," Mr. Helms said.

Mrs. Helms nodded. "Maybe something good will come of this day."

I wondered if she just meant the water. Before I could ask, she called out in a grumpy voice, "Louise, let's go. It's hot and I can't stand being in a car with a bunch of ornery young-uns."

22

Along with magnolias and mint juleps, something often linked with the South was its penchant for making and consuming "moonshine" whisky. I'd never tasted or even seen any of it. The topic came up one day when I was telling Dan about a story I had written about an ATF agent chasing two moonshiners west of Gadsden.

The agent, I believe his name was Hartley, was in hot pursuit of two men whose names were something like Hathaway and Huntley. It was a strange story in that all the figures involved had names starting with the letter *h*. The chase ended with the two fugitives wrecking their car on a tight curve. Neither was hurt, but there were a lot of broken bottles of whisky. The bad guys were put in jail, according to my account.

The next day the ATF agent called and complimented me on the story, saying it was well written.

"There was only one thing really wrong," he said, with a touch of amusement in his voice. "You had me as one of the guys getting put in jail."

Mr. Helms listened closely as I related the tale, including the embarrassing error. Then he asked, "How much whisky was they haulin'?"

"Enough to make the car dip low in the back," I said. "That's how he spotted them."

He thought about it for a while, studying the floor. "There's a place not far from here where a fella gets this moonshine whisky and sells it."

"How do you know that?" Mrs. Helms asked, an irritating note of suspicion in her voice. "Whata you know about moonshinin' and all such as that?"

Mr. Helms shook his head, and when he spoke his voice was a little sharper than usual. "I just know, that's all. I been told that's where they sell it."

"I bet it's been twenty years since you had a sip of moonshine whisky," she said. "Leastways I ain't seen you." Then she muttered darkly to herself, "Course I ain't always seen everything you do. For all I know you might have drank ten gallons of it."

"I ain't touched a drop since I don't recall when," he retorted without rancor. Then he chuckled, and looked at me. "I know when I was in the Army in 1918, I had a bad toothache one night and the sergeant tells me to go see the doctor. So I go to the tent where the doctor stayed, and he got up and looked at my tooth. The jaw was all swelled up. So he tells this sergeant something and says for me to sit and wait. Well, the sergeant comes back in about a hour or so and hands the doctor this bottle of somethin', didn't know what it was. So he gives me the bottle and says to take a drink of the stuff and let it sit on my tooth, and it would help it."

"Was it moonshine?" I asked.

"Yeah, that's what it was," he replied. "I reckon they knowed somebody around here that made the stuff, 'cause they got it in a hurry. I never did know where it came from. But I took the bottle with me, and I would let it numb the tooth for a while, then I'd swallow it. I finally went to sleep. The next day or so they pulled it."

"Must have been high-powered stuff," I said.

With a quick nod Mr. Helms noted, "It helped take care of the toothache and put me to sleep."

"Who sells the stuff around here?" I asked.

"Don't recall his name, but I know where his place is."

Millie asked him to take us there, adding, "I think everyone should taste moonshine whisky at least once in their life."

"You ain't never tasted it?" Minnie asked in a tone of disbelief.

"No, I've never tasted it," Millie said. Then nodding at me, she added, "Neither has he."

"I'm game," I said. "At least for one taste."

Mrs. Helms let the kids stay with her while Dan showed Millie and me the way to a moonshiner's place of business. We drove about five miles along a paved road, then turned onto a dirt-and-gravel lane that ran by green meadows full of lazy-looking cows.

"Watch out, we turn right up yunder there," he said, leaning close from the backseat. "Right there where them tree branches hang down. See it?"

I pulled into a dirt driveway that ran next to a tilting gray barn; it was so old the wood was curling. I started to stop, thinking this was the place. But Mr. Helms told me to keep driving. Soon we were out in an open pasture that had two worn tire paths. It curved by a small shedlike building that also had old graying wood.

"Slow down," he said, staring ahead. "Now stop right by this little building."

The small shanty did not have glass windows, just wood boarding. As soon as I stopped, a half-door opened and a little bald-headed man appeared. He nodded. "Can I hep ya?"

"I guess we want one bottle," I said.

The man handed me a pint bottle containing a clear liquid that looked like water. "Two dollars," he said.

I handed him two ones and he nodded.

"Go on, pull outta here," Mr. Helms urged. "Be our luck to have the law show up."

I swung the car around and fairly flew over the narrow path.

It had crossed my mind that a federal agent could be watching us. It would be funny indeed if I were to be arrested by the agent whom I had mistakenly written into jail.

The moonshine, for my money, had a smooth taste but wasn't any better than what could be purchased legally. I had two drinks, then left the rest for anyone else in the family who wanted to have a taste. The bottle stayed in the refrigerator for a year before someone poured it out.

23

For all her ill moods, Minnie Belle Helms from time to time showed a sense of humor—usually at the expense of someone else. One day Mr. Helms had been working in the back garden. I had helped him set out some squash seed, then had gone in to get a drink of water. As I stood by the well on the back porch, I glanced out and saw him heading for the outhouse.

About that time Mrs. Helms came onto the back porch, got the dipper and helped herself to a drink of water. She saw her husband just as he entered the outhouse. She kept standing there gazing, saying nothing. I was about to go inside the house, when Louise walked out onto the porch.

She and Millie had been in the living room folding clothes.

"Where you a-fixin' to go?" Mrs. Helms asked.

"Gotta go out here," Louise replied. Then she went down the back steps and began the walk down the narrow pathway.

Mrs. Helms took another sip of water from the dipper. She had said nothing about Mr. Helms being in the outhouse. I glanced questioningly at her. Her face was blank, but she kept her eyes on the old gray two-seater as Louise drew nearer.

Then she reached for the door and started to pull it open.

"Whoa!" we heard Mr. Helms call out loudly. "Watch out!"

At the same instant Louise jumped back with a start, then turned around hurriedly. Even from that distance I could see her face was flushed with embarrassment.

Mrs. Helms was cackling, the laughter causing her to spill water on her dress. She had several kinds of laughs. Often it was just a little "hmmp" sound. But when it was something that she thought was really funny, it was "heh-heh-heh." This was one of those.

"Momma!" Louise cried, as she rushed toward the back steps. "You could have told me Daddy was out there."

Mrs. Helms was still chortling, the merriment making her body shake. Finally she blurted out, "You didn't ask me if anyone was out there!"

"Well, you could have said something," Louise said, doing her best to stifle a smile. "It shamed Daddy."

"I just wanted to see what would happen," her mother said, her voice lilting with innocence.

Millie came to the back door. "What's going on?" she inquired.

When she heard the account, she laughed, too. "I guess she got you, Louise."

"Yeah, they got me all right," her sister said. "I guess I'll know to knock the next time I go out there."

Mr. Helms, for his part, was hardly fazed by the episode. At least, that's what he told me. But later in the day, when we were back in the garden and the women were out of earshot, he punched me on the shoulder. That was a sure sign that there was a story coming.

"Talk about somebody being red-faced," he said. "I'll tell you a true story that happened to one fella right around here, but it was back yunder a spell."

"This one's a true story?" I asked.

Mr. Helms nodded, his face serious. "They've all been true stories."

"Well, all right, let's hear it," I said, preparing for a good laugh.

He leaned on the hoe, glanced once more at the house to make sure it was clear, then began.

"This man was taking his family to town one Saturday mornin' and the road ran by this other fella's farm. He had a little pigpen there right by the road. Anyway, the man and his family were in a wagon, and as they came around the pen, they looked and there was the other man standing there. He had his root stuck in a pig. Well, the man in the wagon stopped and looked, and the whole family looked. And the man with the pig, he says, 'That's it. Go to town and tell a bunch of lies about me!' "

He had broken into laughter before completing the last line, and he kept on as he said, "Ain't that somethin'? They caught him dead to rights."

I shook my head. "Yeah. Go to town and tell a bunch of lies. They didn't have to lie about that one."

For sure it was more humiliating than having the outhouse door opened on you.

Later that day, Mrs. Helms again showed some humor. She and her daughters were talking about the Depression years, and Dan and I sat by listening.

Then, chuckling as she began to talk, Minnie said, "I remember one time me and your daddy lived in a old place—I guess you called it a shanty, because it weren't much—and this old fella come by one day lookin' to see if we had any work he could do. Lord, he was so pitiful, his clothes were all in tatters. And"—she started laughing again, then, wiping at her eyes, managed to continue—"his pants was ripped right in front. And he was standin' there and didn't have no idee that his dong was a-hangin' out—" Now she literally broke down with laughter.

Mr. Helms smiled briefly at the memory. Then he shook his head. "Poor fella was wonderin' why Minnie was laughin', but he finally went on his way. I did tell him he needed to get himself another set of britches."

24

October had always been my favorite month, ever since my boyhood in Ohio. There, October meant the trees would turn to flaming scarlet and lavish shades of orange, purple, and yellow. The street where our home was located in Byesville, Ohio, was like a picture from a New England magazine.

Alabama looks different in October; most of the trees remain green until very late in the month. November in this state is like October in Ohio. Regardless, it was my favorite time of year.

But one day in 1964 I came home early on an October afternoon. I was to work that night covering a meeting of some sort. However, arriving at the house, I found Millie lying in the bedroom, and she told me she believed she was going into labor. We didn't have a phone, so I hopped in the green Dodge and drove to Highway 431 to call the doctor. She didn't have an OB-GYN, just a general practitioner we found in the telephone book.

When I told him the situation, he coolly rebuffed me, saying it was probably false labor.

But that evening the pains continued, and Millie had me call Louise. An hour later she and Mrs. Helms arrived, and we headed for the hospital. A neighbor said she would watch the children.

At the hospital a nurse called the doctor, and he reluctantly came in. We sat in the waiting room, saying nothing. I had been through this before, but this time it seemed different.

Moments later we heard a scream that sent a cold chill through my stomach. "That's Millie," I said.

"That was her," Mrs. Helms said grimly. "Somethin' ain't right."

Then we heard someone, a nurse or one of the nuns, crying, "Hurry, call Dr. Nolen, it's an emergency! Hurry!"

I had a devastating feeling of helplessness, and I sat there shaking my head.

A half hour or so passed, and Dr. Jack Nolen came into the room. In a sad voice he told us, "It's a baby boy. It was a very difficult delivery. The baby was turned. It was a breech. We did our best. But the baby's breathing was interrupted for some time. We'll be watching him during the night."

We named him John Daniel. He was born about nine o'clock on October 20. He died at one in the morning of the twenty-first. He never saw a sunrise. Millie asked the nurse if she could hold him for a while. When they brought him in, she cradled him beside her, and I sat there with my hand on his little hand, wishing he would cry out.

It was the worst time of my life. I vaguely remember Mrs. Helms saying to me, "He was just a little fella. It ain't right. He just never had a chance."

In the weeks ahead we would go to Wellington to visit and just get away from the house in Glencoe. Millie was in a deep depression.

On cool autumn days I would go down by the burned-out homesite and fling rocks at trees. One day it drizzled and the air was raw. Mr. Helms came out and watched me. He never said a word, just stood there watching. When my arm grew sore, I turned and walked back to the house. He took one last look at the trees, then came along with me.

He was there to give some support, and the only way he knew was to stand and watch.

25

Christmas that year was bleak. We bought what we could for the children, but it was difficult to enjoy the season.

On Christmas Day evening we rode to Wellington to visit with Mr. and Mrs. Helms. They were in the living room, the gas heater burning orange and blue. A bare lightbulb hanging from the ceiling provided the light. They had put up a small Christmas tree, an artificial one about two feet high. It had no decorations or lights. The place was without cheer.

But we said "Merry Christmas" when we entered, and Dan and Minnie Belle each responded in kind.

There were some cookies and vanilla cake that someone in the family had sent over, and the children devoured most of it. We made coffee and sat in the living room, listening to some carols on the radio.

Mr. Helms was in the rocking chair, his eyes sometimes closing for long seconds. Finally Mrs. Helms scolded, "Dan, are you goin' to sleep?"

He roused himself, shook his head like a riled buffalo, then muttered, "Just restin' my eyes."

"Hummp. You're gonna fall right out of that rocker if you don't watch out." Then she gave a brief snort of a laugh. "If you did it would serve you right."

"Daddy's tired," Millie said.

As for me, I was tired, too. But I was also hungry, and in addition to the cake and cookies, I caught the aroma of something else—fresh-baked bread. I went into the kitchen, and there on the table were two golden-brown loaves. They were still warm.

Risking the wrath of Mrs. Helms, I got a knife and cut off a big piece, put butter on it, then took a bite. It was delicious. Then I walked into the living room.

At first no one seemed to notice. Then Millie asked, "What are you eating?"

"Bread and butter."

Mrs. Helms looked up at me, then drawled, "You didn't get that off the kitchen table, did you?"

I hesitated. "Yeah. Why?"

Then she and Mr. Helms both started laughing.

"What's so funny?" I asked, just a little alarmed. "Something wrong with it?"

"Naw, ain't nothin' wrong with it," she finally said. "It's just that I had made it for the dogs."

Now Millie smiled, and her eyes smiled too. It was the first time since that day in October that I had seen that.

Mrs. Helms shook her head. "All I did is mix flour and water with a little salt," she said. "We'd run out of dog food till the next payday. But I reckon if it's good enough for the hounds, it's good enough for you."

I agreed with her.

Mr. Helms spit snuff into a can and cleared his throat, the signal that he might have a story to tell. And he did.

"One Christmas back yunder around 1928 or so I got a pretty good gift from some corn that we grew," he said. "It was a place we was workin' for shares."

"How'd you do that?" Millie asked.

"Hmmm?"

A long pause. "I said, how did you get a Christmas gift from corn?" she said, smiling at his lapse in memory.

"Well, I had planted some corn seed real late in the season, I think about early September or so," he said, gazing at the flames in the little heater. "Anyway, along about the end of November it had done tasseled and put on ears. But it started gettin' cold, and one day they talked about a freeze comin' that night. I figured I would lose it all. So I got out in the field there and started pullin' up the stalks, one by one. Worked all day. I guess I got four or five hundred stalks pulled up and hauled 'em to the barn. Then I just shoved 'em all in there hard as I could. They was all squashed together in there."

"Did the freeze come?" I asked.

"Yep. But they was in the barn," he said, pausing to think about it. "I just left 'em there. I was figurin' on usin' it to feed the stock, the fodder, you know. But one day just before Christmas, I went in the barn and got lookin' at 'em. Being close together like that kept the heat in, and all them ears had ripened. I tasted one; it tasted just as fresh as if it was in August."

"They were still good?" Millie asked.

Mr. Helms nodded. "So I started pullin' the ears. I piled 'em up in the wagon and carried 'em to town. Must have been eight hundred ears. Left the shucks on 'em. Here it was cold, and even snowin' some. And I had them fresh ears of corn. The store bought most of 'em from me. I sold the rest of 'em that day to people comin' by. Don't remember what I sold 'em for, but I made about forty-five or fifty dollars, somethin' like that."

"Pretty shrewd," Millie observed.

Mrs. Helms nodded. "Well, that was a right smart amount of money back then. I tell you it was."

26

On January 2, 1965, the University of Alabama played Texas in the Orange Bowl. The next day newspapers devoted a lot of space to the heroic efforts of Alabama quarterback Joe Namath, who, although limping with a bad knee, almost scored a touchdown in the final moments. But Texas held on and won.

There was little attention paid to an event in Selma, Alabama. The Reverend Martin Luther King Jr. made a speech at Brown Chapel AME Church, kicking off what he said was the start of a voting rights drive to get black people registered in rural counties in the state and across the South.

Within weeks the news wires were humming with stories about Selma. Now Gadsden is about 150 miles northeast of Selma, and what was happening there was not of direct concern to the management of the *Gadsden Times.*

One day I asked the new executive editor if I could go to Selma and write a story.

His reply was simple. "Our job is to cover local news. We've got the AP and UPI to handle stories in other parts of the state. You cover the police, the city hall, and the courthouse. That's local. That's your job."

The mood of most whites in Alabama at that time was to be against just about anything that was backed by the federal government. The attitude was manifested by the Confederate flag that flew atop the state capitol in Montgomery. There were other signs, as well. WVOK, a popular Birmingham radio station, signed off at sundown with a stirring martial version of "Dixie," and later at night WAAX in Gadsden went off the air with a choral version of the same song:

"O I wish I was in the land of cotton,
Old times there are not forgotten.
Look away, look away,
Look away, Dixieland."

In early February the Gadsden Chamber of Commerce announced that Governor Wallace was coming to town on the nineteenth to give the keynote address for what was known as "Salute to Gadsden Industry," and they hoped for a lot of media coverage. Wallace, of course, was the South's number one leader in the region's battle to stymie desegregation. His inauguration speech in January 1963 defined his stance: "Segregation today, segregation tomorrow, segregation forever!" Of course, Gadsden city leaders were not viewing his visit in terms of racial politics but rather in terms of the progress the city had made in industry, jobs, and dollars. But, aware that race was something that hovered about the state, the planners made certain that Wallace would visit a black trade school, where he could announce a state grant to help the programs there.

Mayor Les Gilliland told me he hoped the *New York Times* and all three of the national TV networks would send someone to cover the event. Gilliland, a short, intense man with a brush haircut and glasses, was a fair-minded individual and, in my opinion, probably a liberal at heart. I was surprised to see John Kennedy's inaugural message posted on the wall behind his desk.

But I believed he was misguided in thinking the national news media was coming to Gadsden for a Chamber of Commerce event. They all had crews in Selma.

Meantime, the center of attention moved from Selma to Marion, the seat of Perry County, about twenty-eight miles west of Selma. There, tension had been smoldering between civil rights activists and local white leaders. Marches had been held, and some marchers were jailed. A rally was slated for February 18. Some Selma marchers drove there to join in. At the same time, Wallace ordered Alabama state troopers to assist local law enforcement. A meeting was held in a church, and when the black group came out, they decided to march down the street to the jail, just a block away. Troopers blocked the attempt, and soon it turned into a melee. During the encounter some of the reporters were beaten, cameras sprayed with black paint, and lights shot out. A black woodcutter, Jimmie Lee Jackson, twenty-seven, was shot by a trooper during a struggle in a cafe.

It was a major national story the next morning, and the news media came in a pack looking for Governor Wallace—who was to be in Gadsden at noon that day. The coverage that the mayor had hoped for was coming—but not for the reasons he had planned.

Most of the news staff of the *Gadsden Times,* including me, was sent to the luncheon meeting. My role was to cover for the Associated Press, as well as for United Press International.

I was dressed in my hand-me-down brown suit that had been obtained at a thrift store. It was too baggy. To make matters worse, I had just gotten a haircut. The barber, an elderly man with palsy, had not only trimmed my hair around the edges but, because of his shaking hands, had cut a wide swath on the right back of my head, which contrasted sharply with the longer hair hanging down from my crown. I didn't know about it, and no one told me.

After Wallace's speech about industry and progress in Alabama, the floor was opened to questions from the news media.

The first question from a TV reporter was something like this: "Governor, what is your response to charges that your state troopers beat peaceful marchers in Marion last night?"

Wallace dodged the issue by saying he was not sure what had happened and that he was still looking into the matter.

The TV reporter pressed the governor: "Will you comment on the fact that a trooper shot one of the marchers?"

By now the diners began to react, and a wave of muttered discontent rippled over the ballroom, things such as "Sit down," and

"We're not here for that." A former police chief angrily gestured to me. I edged closer to him.

"Who is that guy asking those questions?" he demanded.

"Don't know," I said. Actually, I didn't know him personally, but I knew who he was.

Later, after the meeting ended, I went up on the stage to ask some further questions of Wallace about the incident in Marion. When I introduced myself, he looked at me suspiciously, slowly unwrapping a cigar and lighting it. "You're with who?" he snapped irritably.

"The *Times,*" I said.

"The *Times*!" he cried, his eyes quickly scanning the ill-fitting brown suit. I knew what he was thinking: this guy can't be with the *New York Times.*

"The *Gadsden Times,*" I quickly clarified.

"Oh." He puffed on the cigar. "What's your question?"

A photographer snapped a picture of me talking with the governor. The swath on my head was an absolute glare. No wonder Wallace was so elusive in dealing with me.

The situation in Alabama was growing more intense by the hour. On February 25 Jackson died at Good Samaritan Hospital in Selma. More marches were planned.

Mrs. Waller brought her column in one afternoon, and she was obviously distressed.

"A lot of us are very concerned about what's going on," she said, her voice low. She leaned forward and in a confidential tone added, "You see, it's not just in Selma. But what happens there and in Marion affects us all. There's a lot of talk in our community about some kind of show of support here. Some are talking about demonstrating. It is very upsetting. We don't know what to expect."

"I'm sure it will all work itself out in time," I said, trying to assure her.

A phone rang at the desk behind me, and I swung around for a moment. When I turned back Mrs. Waller's expression had relaxed. There was even a trace of a smile.

She probably wondered where I got the haircut.

27

Like everyone else in Alabama, Dan and Minnie Belle Helms had their opinions about what was happening in the state and what was the cause.

"It's that King fella, the way I see it," he said. We were sitting on the front porch. He had his spit can with him beside the rocker. "If he'd stayed at home where he belonged, nothin' would've happened down there. And he's supposed to be a preacher. Gets me why them folks listen to him. They just don't learn nothin'. They keep on."

Mrs. Helms, on the swing with Millie, shook her head and squinted through the glasses. "Don't make no sense to me why they always marchin' and carryin' on, nohow. Why they doin' it for?"

Millie shrugged. "Voting rights, they say."

"Votin' rights," Mrs. Helms snorted. "Who votes anyway? I don't recall the last time I ever voted. It don't mean nothin' nohow. Them ones in Montgomery or Washington or wherever are gonna do what they want, no matter. I don't even bother."

"If you decide not to vote, Mother, that's your right," Millie said casually. "But you and I do have the right to go vote if we want. The Negro people don't have that right, and they should have it. They shouldn't have to march to be able to vote. Don't you think?"

"Well, who in the world's tryin' to keep 'em from votin'?" her mother demanded, eyes narrow. "It ain't me."

"I guess it's our state laws and some people who work at courthouses," Millie said. "I don't really know."

Mr. Helms spit into the can, wiped tobacco juice from his chin, and muttered, "I heard tell some of 'em can vote. I know there are some colored preachers in Anniston who vote. I been told that."

"See there," Mrs. Helms said. "If they'd put their minds to it, they could do it."

Millie shook her head. Not wanting to argue with her mother, she looked at me to offer some explanation.

"As I understand it, some can vote in the cities and some towns," I said. "But in some of the rural counties the voting registrars give these tests and not many Negroes pass them. Mrs. Waller says she can vote, but she said in some places the tests have questions that are crazy."

"Like what?" Millie asked.

"Well, things like how many bubbles in a bar of soap." I'd heard that.

Mrs. Helms gave a grunt. "That ain't crazy, that's plain silly. No one can answer that. Not and get it right to suit someone."

"So wouldn't that make you mad?" Millie asked her.

Mrs. Helms stood up and shook her head. "I don't know nothin'," she said in an unsteady voice. "I got more things to worry me than goin' to vote, I can tell you that." She walked to the front door, opened it and gazed in. Then, without looking at us, she declared, "It don't bother me if nary a nigger ever votes, or all of 'em vote. Don't bother me a bit one way or the other."

And she entered the house and slammed the door.

I had had to take a voting test when I registered in Gadsden. It involved nothing more than copying a sentence from the Declaration of Independence.

28

The Selma marches peaked on Sunday, March 7, 1965, at the Edmund Pettus Bridge, when about 625 marchers tried to make a pilgrimage to Montgomery. The group leaders said they wanted to meet with Governor Wallace.

State troopers charged into the file of marchers and began striking them as they scrambled wildly in retreat. Later teargas canisters were rolled among the marchers. That night the nation watched the black-and-white footage on TV. The reaction was shock, disbelief, and outrage.

Americans from all walks of life flocked to Selma to take part in follow-up marches and to be part of the history that was unfolding. On Tuesday, March 9, a Unitarian minister, James Reeb, thirty-eight, of Boston, was struck on the head by a group of angry white men. He died two days later.

That day Harriet Waller came to the office of the *Times,* and I could see she had been crying.

I asked what was wrong, although I knew fairly well.

"There's going to be a march here," she said. "We're so afraid, some of us. We're afraid of how things can get so out of hand, that someone could be killed. You probably don't understand the way I feel. I wish they would stay at home, but they're talking about a march, and I know they are going to do it."

She was right. The next day we received a news release announcing a march. Gadsden was going to have a march just as dozens of other cities and towns across America were going to have them, to show support for the voting drive in Selma. It seemed the whole world was watching Alabama and Selma. *Time* magazine wrote that "Selma was no longer just a place, but a state of mind."

The march in Gadsden saw more than one thousand blacks turn out on a cool but sunny day. I walked alongside the column as it moved to the city hall and asked a young woman why she was there that day.

"For freedom," she replied, her voice showing surprise that such a question should be asked. "And to show the people in Selma we stand behind them."

I asked the new police chief, L. E. Hamrick, what his instructions were to his men as the marchers came to the city hall.

"We are here to provide protection for citizens who are exercising a right," he said, which I thought was a surprisingly revealing statement.

Then the marchers reached city hall, a new building that overlooked the Coosa River. Office workers peered out from behind the tinted windows. The group sang "We Shall Overcome."

It was the first time I'd ever heard it sung. It touched an emotional chord in me, a realization that I was a witness to a small part of history. A newspaper reporter is to be impartial, I was told. But hearing those people sing that song with such feeling made it difficult to walk the center line.

After some speeches from ministers the groups peacefully began the walk back to their rally point, a church on the northwest side of the city. Going through the downtown I saw what could have been an ugly incident.

As the marchers went by a place where an alley intersected Broad Street, two young white men in a red car had stopped. The driver suddenly lurched the car forward, forcing some of the blacks to jump into the street to avoid being hit. A police officer happened to be walking close by. He hurried to the spot and shouted, "Back that thing up!"

The driver, who had been laughing, became sober-faced and eased the vehicle farther into the alley.

I figured the police officer was not sympathetic with the march, but, at the same time, he didn't want any problems to occur, knowing it would bring the eyes of the nation down on Gadsden.

However, the eyes stayed on Selma; a few days later U.S. District Judge Frank M. Johnson Jr. issued an order allowing civil rights marchers to walk from Selma to Montgomery to dramatize the need for a voting rights bill. The march was to be held March 21, 1965.

29

The next time we went to Wellington, I said nothing about the racial situation in the state because we had been over that ground time and again. Nothing would be solved by getting into a debate with Millie's parents. I knew where they stood, and I didn't want to get them upset.

But to my surprise Mr. Helms brought it up as I was watching the kids play outside under the water oak.

"Where was that place them police took to beatin' on them colored folks?" he asked.

"Selma."

"Where?"

"Selma. Remember, we drove through there one morning when we came back from Florida," I reminded him.

We had taken a wrong turn in Montgomery and took U.S. 80 west to Selma instead of heading north on U.S. 231. We had passed through Selma at about 4 a.m. That was in March 1961.

He nodded, as he remembered. Then, frowning and shaking his head, he inquired, "Why were they out there paradin' around in the first place? They was askin' for trouble, if you ask me."

"A lot of people are going down there for the march to Montgomery Sunday," I said. Then I looked down the road at the house where the black family lived. "I wonder if any of those folks are going? You heard?"

"Ain't heard nary a word," he replied, glancing down at the house. "Don't know what they're doin'. We don't nose into their business, and they mind their own as far as what we do. But it seems a lot of them from all over are goin' down there. Leastways I heard they was."

"There's a church bus from Gadsden going down," I said.

Mr. Helms nodded. "I think it was yesterday Robert was gettin' some gas down yunder and he said this colored fella pulls up in a big car and asks how to get to that place you just said—"

"Selma."

"Yeah, Selma." Mr. Helms paused to collect his thoughts. "Anyway, I reckon Robert told him the way, 'cause he had been a-headin' in the wrong direction at the time. He had New York plates on his car."

"Long drive," I said.

"Yep. Long ways. I don't reckon I'd go that far just to walk to Montgomery, would you?"

I shrugged. "I guess it depends."

He turned to spit, wiped at his chin, then peered down toward the house on the other side of the tracks. We could see a number of black children running about, their laughter rising and falling.

"Makes you wonder," he said.

At that moment we saw Louise's car making the turn by the towering pine. We watched as she pulled to a halt and some of the children alighted. Then she got out.

"How y'all?" she called.

"We're just out here a-gabbin'," Mr. Helms said, with a grin.

"What you gabbin' about?"

"We were talking about that march they're going to have Sunday, from Selma to Montgomery," I said.

She paused. "I heard something about that on the radio." She took another step toward us, stopped and folded her arms, looking directly at me. "Well, I'll just tell you, I believe they should allow them to vote, and go to places to eat and such as that, but I don't think they should force our kids to go to school with them. That's just how I feel, and I don't care who knows it."

And with that she went into the house. Mr. Helms nodded but said nothing.

From down the road we heard a squeal as the children at Rosie Wood's house continued their play.

"Sounds like they are having a good time," I said.

Mr. Helms squinted at the house. Then, raising his eyebrows and smiling just a little, he said, "Young-uns always have a good time, no matter what's goin' on, I reckon."

30

In late 1965 we moved from Glencoe to a newer home in Gadsden. It was one of a number of houses the government had built in the early 1950s. The subdivision was called Oakleigh Estates, and for some reason most of the houses were empty. I figured it was because the federal government was funding the project.

The world was changing around us. The conflict in Vietnam, which had started with little notice, had grown into a full-scale war. Several young men from the Gadsden area were killed there, and I covered their funerals. There was an eerie sameness about them. Each time there was a death, I would visit the family home and talk with the parents. They would show me the last letter their son had written them. Almost all of them read the same, ending with a line that went something like this: "Don't worry about me. The Lord will watch over me."

The one that struck the deepest chord with me was a Marine named Auburn Foreman, twenty-two. When we received word of his death in December 1965, I called the family to ask permission to talk with them and also get a photograph.

A sister, Gail Oden, came to our office. I will never forget the look of absolute devastation on her face. Her dark eyes had a haunted, bewildered look about them, as through she could not fully comprehend that her brother had been killed.

I stood up when she entered. She handed me the picture of a smiling young man with close-cropped red hair.

"Did they tell you how my brother was killed?" she asked, her voice sparse, hollow.

I shook my head. "No, ma'am."

She sat down beside my desk. "His unit was in a back area, getting a few days of rest. We had sent him his Christmas presents. He was sitting on an open hillside opening the presents. And a U.S. helicopter flew overhead. And I guess the pilot thought Auburn was an enemy soldier. He fired his rockets and one hit right beside Auburn. It killed him. He was killed by mistake."

To add irony to the grief, a few days later Mrs. Oden and her children received some gifts that had been sent by her brother the day before he was killed.

I told Mr. Helms about it one day, and he shook his head sadly.

"Reckon it was like that in all the wars," he said. "Poor boys. They all was a-thinkin' the Lord was goin' to keep 'em from gettin' killed. Folks around here got letters like that in the First World War, and some got 'em in the second one. Then they got letters in—what'd they call that other place?"

"Korea. The Korean War."

"Yeah, that's right."

He shifted the snuff about in his mouth, so he could talk more clearly, blinking slowly as he collected his thoughts.

"Back in World War Two this place was full of folks, comin' and goin' to and from that train station." He nodded toward the white structure with green trim. It was now silent. "That train station was where all them soldiers would come to when they was goin' to the fort over here [Fort McClellan]. And when they'd leave to go overseas, they'd have to come back through here. Lot of traffic in them days. Now there ain't nothin'. But I reckon a lot of them soldiers probably got killed over there, and I bet every one of 'em wrote a letter home like the ones you talked about."

I nodded. "That's probably true."

"Yeah, it's true," he said. "Anyway, I reckon it's always the same in every blamed war we get into." He spat again, shook his head, then declared, "Prayin' won't stop a bullet."

"You don't think it does any good to pray?"

He fixed a hard gaze on me and spoke loudly: "I sure do. But I think the Lord, He has it all planned out, and all that goes on is set out in His plan. When it's your time, it's your time, and that's 'cause that's how He planned it."

31

In August 1967 I took a job with the *Birmingham News,* which meant our visits with Millie's parents grew further apart. We'd see them mostly during summer vacation periods or holidays. I took the job because it offered higher pay, and it was a step up, going to the biggest paper in the state. And besides, we had our sixth child, Janet, who came in June 1966.

The work schedule at the *News* called for me to be in the office by 6:15; I seldom got off at 3:15. One evening in April 1968 I didn't get home until after six, and I was still at the kitchen table with a TV dinner in front of me when Debbie, who was now twelve, hurried into the living room.

"Hey, Dad," she called. "Somebody shot that Reverend King. It's on TV next door."

At first I didn't quite believe it. But she had told me the news about John Kennedy back in 1963. Now it was King. We turned on the TV and sure enough, the news was on that Martin Luther King Jr. had been assassinated in Memphis.

Moments later the telephone rang, and an assistant editor at the *News* told me, "Be ready to come in if anything happens. There could be some problems here."

That night there was rioting reported in some cities as angry blacks spilled into the streets. Birmingham, however, remained relatively quiet.

But the next day it began to simmer. I was sent to city hall. Shortly before noon reports began coming in of large groups of blacks gathering at different sites, apparently prepared to march on the downtown. Police radios crackled with updates.

Left to right: Victor, Terry, and Frankie standing; Debbie seated; and Millie holding Janet, 1966.

In the early afternoon about two thousand people gathered in Kelly Ingram Park, a rallying point for marches led by King in 1963. I observed the crowd from across the street, standing near a police officer and two men who appeared to be FBI agents.

A man was speaking from a small platform, and the crowd was reacting to his words. Then, suddenly, a shiny streak sailed over the crowd and hit near another group of reporters and officers. As though a signal had been given, the crowd shrieked and burst into a mad scramble in all directions. I joined the police officer and the FBI guys, turning and running at top speed. Then we stopped a half block away. The crowd had dispersed into small groups of three or four people.

The demonstration was over. The only violent act was someone throwing a soda bottle at the reporters. It missed. A day later there was a memorial service held at Lynn Park, near the city hall.

The next time we visited the folks in Wellington Mrs. Helms was quick to comment about the King murder.

"I don't reckon that colored preacher will be a-leadin' any more marches," she said. Then: "He'd a-been better off stayin' at home and mindin' his own church."

We didn't respond. Mr. Helms thought about it, then shook his head.

"I don't hold with killin' a man for speakin' his mind," he said. "But he oughta knowed somebody might try shootin' at him if he stayed out there long enough. He oughta knowed."

Millie shrugged. "The world's full of crazy people."

"And there gets to be more of 'em everyday," Mrs. Helms added, slapping her hand on the chair arm for emphasis. "No, I don't hold with killin' either, but I was just a-sayin' he would still be alive if he'd stayed closer to his own church."

Mr. Helms pulled his lip out and took a fresh dip of snuff. Then, getting it situated right, he said, "Well, didn't I hear 'em say on TV that they traced that gun to some store in Birmingham?"

That was true, I said.

"Reckon it was somebody from there that done it?" Mrs. Helms asked.

"Might have been," Millie said. "A lot of people in Birmingham probably didn't like him."

"They had a whole lot on the news about it," Mr. Helms commented. "Seems to me he'd have been better off not gettin' mixed up in that mess. What was they? Garbage workers?"

We nodded. "Garbage workers," Millie said. "In Memphis."

Mr. Helms shook his head. "It keeps on and before long we'll be in a sure-enough war amongst each other."

"Be like the Civil War," Millie agreed.

The Civil War . . .

The mention of it seemed to draw a cloak of silence over the room. I waited for someone to say something, because I knew there had been a connection between the Helms family and the war. Every southern family had some connection. So I waited. Presently, Mr. Helms cleared his throat, moved the snuff about, nodded, then spoke:

"My daddy's cousin fought in that war. Went up into Virginia, then ended up down here other side of where Gadsden is. The war was about over and he ended up there. Didn't have no horse, didn't have much of nothin'. Didn't even have shoes. So he walks barefoot on to where his folks was stayin' and as he was walkin' by the Coosa River he threw his pistol in the water."

"Why'd he do that?" I asked.

"Huh?"

"I said why did he throw his gun into the river?"

"Why, shoot, man," he scoffed, "he done that so them Yankees wouldn't catch him with a gun. If they did, they'd likely kill him or take him off. They was everywhere. He didn't want 'em to know he'd been fightin' against 'em."

In March 1969 Millie had a baby girl we named Michelle. When we visited Wellington a month or so later, Mr. Helms took the baby and held her on his knee, bouncing her up and down softly and humming a tune that I could never make out. Mrs. Helms held her, too, although she seemed to be less enthused about it.

In late July a special election was held in Greene County; blacks won, making it the first time since Reconstruction that their race held control of any county government in Alabama—and probably anywhere in the South. It was history. The *News* sent me there, and I carried a camera.

On July 31 the official recount was held in the courthouse, a white structure that looked like Alabama in the 1840s or so. It was a beautiful place. Inside where the counting was taking place, Sheriff Bill Lee, a 240-pound, ruddy-faced man, sat quietly, smoking a pipe. He had one arm thrown over the empty seat next to him. As I stood watching, the Reverend Ralph Abernathy, King's successor as head of the Southern Christian Leadership Conference, eased into the seat by the sheriff.

A second later I walked closer, focused the 120-mm Yashica, and snapped a picture. Lee did not move and continued to sit with a benevolent expression, the pipe clenched between his teeth.

Several weeks later I saw Sheriff Lee, and he grinned but said in a low voice, "You son of a gun, you trapped me. When Abernathy sat down next to me I just couldn't move my arm." Then he slapped me on the shoulder. "I'm running for re-election next year, and I might want to buy that picture and use it in my campaign, because I know I'll be running against a black guy."

Lee bought the picture from the *News* and did use it in his 1970 campaign. But he lost to Tom Gilmore.

32

After I'd spent the better part of two weeks in Greene County, the *News* gave me a day off, which I combined with a weekend. We decided to drive to Panama City, Florida, and enjoy the waters of the Gulf of Mexico and the sun.

We planned to leave after work on Friday night, August 15. Unknown to me, two things were happening. First, Millie invited her parents to go with us, and second, Hurricane Camille had battered Cuba and was coming into the Gulf. I learned about Camille when some of my coworkers heard I was going to the beach.

When I arrived home that night, I found Mr. and Mrs. Helms sitting in the kitchen. Millie had gone to pick them up that afternoon.

"I reckon we're a-goin' with you," Mrs. Helms announced, noting my surprise.

Well, what could I say? "It'll be fun if you like riding in a car with a bunch of ornery young-uns." Plus, Michelle was only five months old.

We left that night and stopped in Montgomery, resuming our journey Saturday morning, August 16. As we rode along I turned on the radio. The news was on, and it was all about Camille. The hurricane was located 350 miles southwest of Panama City, and the winds were—static blurred the final words.

"Did he say winds of 115 miles an hour?" I asked.

"He said 150," Millie replied.

Winds of 150 miles an hour? And it was headed for Panama City, the place we were going to stay? Actually, at that point things looked great. The sun was out, hot and bright; only a few fluffy white clouds were seen. But they were moving across the sky at a good clip.

"Maybe we better rethink what we're doing," I said. "That's a mighty strong hurricane. I don't want to be there with the kids when that thing hits."

"It ain't a good place to be," Mr. Helms added from the backseat. "I been in a couple of them things and they was bad. And I was way inland a-piece. Tree limbs fallin'; roofs comin' off. It ain't a good place."

"Well, Dan," said Mrs. Helms, "I ain't never been to the ocean, not once. I ain't leaving 'til I at least get my feet wet. I just want to walk in there one time."

Well, I figured we could at least spend the day there before deciding if we had to leave. So we reached Panama City and checked in at a midpriced motel, across U.S. 98 from the beach. Then we hurried down to the water, the kids diving into the surf, which was already more active than usual because of the storm some 350 miles out in the Gulf.

Then Mrs. Helms came down with Millie. She wore her dress but did take off her shoes. With Millie on one arm and Debbie on the other, she waded into the surf, laughing as she staggered a bit. "It makes me a little dizzy," she called. "That water just rushes by so fast. This is all I wanted to do. Just to be able to say one time I put my feet in the ocean."

After a minute or two, she'd had enough, and they went out. The sun was hot, breaking through the high, splotchy clouds that paraded across the sky. Then Mrs. Helms was ready to go back to the air-conditioned comfort of the motel room. She had waded in the Gulf of Mexico. She was probably the first member of her immediate family to have done so.

Actually, I didn't know it at the time, but it was going to be a historic weekend in America. Camille was coming, and before long nearly two hundred thousand people would flee inland. It would be the second-most-powerful hurricane on record. At the same time, about a half million people were gathering on a farm in upstate New York near a place called Woodstock. I only knew about that later by reading of it.

I walked around the beach area, talked to a few business people as well as tourists, then filed a short story from Panama City saying they were bracing for a possible strike by a potent hurricane. Then we stayed up drinking coffee and watching TV all night. At the time you could only pick up one channel, and it carried the unsettling reports of Camille's potential for visiting rage wherever it struck. The winds were now up to an incredible 190 miles an hour. But the storm's center was stalled in the central Gulf. And no one was sure where it would go.

Millie and Mrs. Helms thought it was exciting. But Mr. Helms and I talked privately and decided that if Camille was heading our way, we were moving out at first light.

By Sunday morning the waves of the Gulf were breaking over the piers; gale force winds were whistling over the beaches, and the sky was a deep charcoal gray. It was scary. But now the hurricane was moving slowly northward, apparently taking aim on Mississippi's coast. I received a telephone call from John Bloomer, the managing editor of the *News,* who told me to prepare to cover the storm if it hit Panama City. I told him I had my family with me.

"Bring your family inland and then go back to cover it," Bloomer said.

But Camille kept on its northerly track and struck the Mississippi coast that night, August 17, with 200-mph winds; it killed 150 people in Mississippi, then later in the week set off flooding in West Virginia and Virginia that killed another 80. I drove the family back to Birmingham early Monday and later went to Mississippi. It looked like the place had been bombed.

33

In 1970 George Wallace made another run for governor. He had not been able to run in 1966 because of a state law that forbade a governor to hold two consecutive terms. Instead, his wife, Lurleen, ran, and she won going away. But not long after the election, doctors discovered she had cancer, and she struggled for two years before dying in May 1968. The lieutenant governor, Albert Brewer, assumed the office. Now he and Wallace were the leaders in a field of several candidates. Primary election day was May 5, 1970.

One evening we drove up to Wellington and had supper with Louise and Robert. Of course, Mr. and Mrs. Helms were there.

Afterward, Mr. Helms and Robert went to the front porch. I joined them. For a while they talked about the weather. Then I changed the topic. I asked Robert if he was going to vote for Wallace.

He was squatted down, smoking a Camel. When I asked the question, his head snapped sharply toward me and his eyes narrowed.

"Francis, I'd vote for the blackest nigger before I'd vote for George Wallace," he said.

I was surprised. "You're not a Wallace man?"

"Hell, no," he said. "I voted for him back in sixty-two. But I'll never vote for him again."

"Why's that?"

"Because he lied," Robert declared. "He lied about keeping black people out of the schools and the colleges. He said he'd stand up to the government and keep them out. But he backed down. He lied."

"So you'll probably vote for Brewer, huh?"

He gave me one of those looks that says it was none of my business. But, he finally spoke: "I ain't made up my mind. But I know it won't be Wallace."

Mr. Helms was listening thoughtfully. Then he volunteered, "I don't reckon I'll even go there and vote. It don't much matter who gets in. Leastways, I don't see much difference in any of 'em."

"There ain't," said Robert. "They all talk a good game, but in the end they're all about the same."

Robert gazed out across the meadow that lay on the other side of the road. Then he flicked the cigarette out into the yard, reached into his pocket and got another one out. When he lit it, he glanced at me, and his expression mellowed.

"Naw, I just get tired of the politicians who say what they're gonna do, and then don't never do it," he said. "Wallace probably ain't no worse than the others. But he shouldn't have been saying things he knew he couldn't back up. I just can't trust someone who'd do that-a-way."

Mr. Helms listened and nodded, then, almost with a start, he started checking his shirt pockets. I thought he might have misplaced some money.

"Durn," he said. "I reckon I'm out of Copenhagen. I forgot to stop and get some."

Robert laughed, then held out his pack of Camels. "You want to try one of these, Mr. Helms?"

"Naw, it ain't the same," he muttered, his face showing a trace of irritation. "I thought at first I might have lost it, but I remembered I was out. Should have stopped at Yaikow's." Then, with a heavy sigh, he turned to the front door. "I'll see if Minnie's got some to lend me."

As Mr. Helms entered the house, Robert grinned at me. "Gotta have his snuff."

"Yeah," I said. "Kinda like you gotta have your Camels. How long you been smoking?"

"Since I was about twelve," he replied quickly. "Way back there.

I started rollin' my own. Bull Durham, Bugler, brands like that. I still smoke some of them once in a while. But mostly it's Camels."

Now Dan returned, his mouth set in a tight line, a sign that he had succeeded in borrowing some of his wife's snuff.

"Well, Mr. Helms, how long you been using tobacco?" Robert asked.

He thought a moment, then said, "I reckon I been usin' tobacco since I was big enough to plow behind a mule. Never smoked it much. Just chewed it or used snuff. Been usin' snuff for forty years or more, I reckon."

Robert shook his head slightly and smiled. "I reckon everybody in the Army smoked when I went in during World War Two. They even issued us cigarettes. They tried to get me to quit once when I got pneumonia on New Guinea. One doctor took my pack. But the chief doctor came by and asked me, 'Soldier, where are your cigarettes?' And I told him the young doctor took them. The head doctor made him give them back. Said I'd be too nervous without them, but as soon as I lit one, I'd put them down. And he was right. I didn't touch another one till I was well."

Mr. Helms nodded. "I reckon if they tried to take snuff away from me, I'd go vote somebody out."

34

Dan Helms never said things that were poetic, but I could tell that when spring came it meant a whole new world for him. He had seen a lot of springtimes, but the one at hand was always the best. His first priority was the garden. It actually started in late January, days when snow flurries sometimes flew and the ground crunched under his boots.

First he tended to the tools he kept in an old shed that sat near the little dog pen. He would scrape them, put oil on some, and sharpen others. Once, when it was still snowing and a crisp wind was blowing, he was out there testing his ax on some old scrub pine that had popped up near the far side of the garden. Then, when the winds settled, he would tromp out into the garden and rake up piles of dead leaves, vines, and stalks, put them in a heap, and burn them. He would stand there, leaning on the rake, intently studying the circles of smoke rising into the chill afternoon sky. He said it helped kill out the eggs that some of the bugs had left behind, waiting for the next growing season. But it seemed to me that he viewed it almost like some ancient Celtic ritual, a spiritual awakening.

Sometimes he would turn his attention away from the fire and look beyond to the tilted picket fence in the adjoining yard, its boundaries marked off by the lines of greens that were emerging. In Alabama the daffodils and jonquils begin bursting out as early as the first of February, sometimes even late in January.

He still spaded the garden by himself, saying it wasn't big enough to pay a man and his mule to do it. I would pitch in and help him when I was there, but he preferred handling it himself. There is nothing quite like the aroma of fresh-turned earth to get a soul prepared for the spring. He never said anything about it, but I figured that's what he was thinking about.

By the first of March he already had some potatoes and onions making strong stands in the lower end of the side garden. A few weeks later he would put in the first planting of beans and corn; when the corn was about four inches high, he would drop some squash seeds among the rows, which is how the Indians did it.

I stood by him one April day; he was in his own world. He was watching (and, I believe, listening to) his garden grow. He placed one hand on the oak tree and leaned slightly as he observed, his eyes narrowed, but his face relaxed in an expression of peace and calm. In the branches above, a robin pranced about on a limb, wondering what there was to see.

"Does Mrs. Helms ever help you with the garden?" I asked.

He thought about it for a moment. "Way back yunder we all had to pitch in. She helped a bit then. But it's been some years, I reckon." Then he gave a grunt of a laugh. "She tells me when I go out, I'd best be getting it all done or she'll lock me out."

"Sort of gives you a chance to get out by yourself," I noted.

He nodded. "I like to come out and mess around every now and again. But sometimes I don't do nothin' but look. This here is the first garden that's ever been ours. We never owned our own place before. Always had to rent. They'd take the rent out of our shares that we helped grow in the fields." Then he gestured toward the garden. "It means a whole lot more when it belongs to you."

Years earlier, Dan and Minnie Belle Helms had gone to church, mostly to those that had tent revivals or held ceremonies along slippery creek banks, where feet were washed and souls cleansed. They had joined the Bethlehem Baptist Church, located east of Oxford but had not attended services there in many years. That afternoon as we were driving home, I asked Millie about it.

She stared at the highway. "I remember when I was little, Daddy and Mother would take me, James, and Louise to some preachings that were in tents. I would get a headache. It would go on for hours."

I shook my head in sympathy. "They don't talk much about church, at least not that I've heard."

"No, although Daddy will sometimes quote a passage from the Bible," she said. "He can't read, but he can remember things like that." Then she added, "I don't know about Mother, but I believe when Daddy is in his garden, he is as close to the Lord as anybody who goes to a church."

35

The spring of 1971 saw one of Mr. Helms's best gardens ever. The turtle and the rabbits and the slugs and all other such critters stayed clear, and he brought along a bumper crop of string beans, squash, corn, tomatoes, and watermelons. By July the melons were nearly ripe for picking, and we'd already feasted on some roasting ears.

Things were so good, in fact, that he allowed that he would put in another planting of beans and still beat the first frost by two weeks or more.

On the first Sunday in August we talked about riding up to Wellington for a visit, maybe even go to Hammonds Creek for a swim. But there was so much to do at the house that we decided not to. Millie called and talked to them and said we'd probably drive up the following Sunday.

On Monday morning I went to work and was preparing to go to a rural section of Alabama for a story. Then the phone rang.

It was Millie. All she said was, "Can you come home? Daddy died this morning. He died in his garden."

We drove to Wellington in silence. By the time we arrived at the house, the roadside was lined with cars of family members and distant relatives.

I thought how strange the place seemed, such a void, knowing old Mr. Helms was not going to be there anymore. But at the same time, it occurred to me that he had died in his garden, the place he'd probably want to spend his last moments. He was eighty-two.

Inside Mrs. Helms was almost in hysterics, crying loudly and trying to talk at the same time. For the first time in my life I felt sorry for her. She was so alone now.

"He was out there hoeing them beans," she wailed. "He'd been there about a half hour or so. Oh my Lord. It is so pitiful. But I looked out once and I saw he was sittin' down under that apple tree, and I reckoned he was just a-restin'. But a little later, I went to get me a drink of water on the back porch, and I looked again and he was a-layin' on his side there. I called, 'Dan, are you all right?' And he just never answered. And that's when I called Louise. But I knowed he was dead. I just knowed it."

The coroner had ruled it was a heart attack. That conclusion brought added distress to Millie.

"I remember seeing Daddy taking Tums or Rolaids all the time," she said. "He thought it was indigestion. I'll bet it was his heart all along and nobody knew it."

The funeral home had already picked up the body. The plan was for him to be brought back home for visitation the next day, followed by the funeral at Bethlehem Baptist Church, where the family had a plot in the church cemetery.

By then neighbors were sending over food, and we stayed through the night.

The next afternoon they brought him back home, dressed in a gray suit. Family members packed the living room and spilled out onto the front porch. It was a hot day, very much like the first day I had come here years before. But this time there was the low rumble of thunder far off. And more distant came the wail of a train. One of the dogs out back began to howl.

I was standing with Robert on the front porch when one of the boys called from the front yard, "Uncle Robert, whose that comin' here?"

Down the road toward the train station was the figure of a black woman walking slowly toward us. Robert puffed on his cigarette in deep thought, apparently trying to place her.

"She ain't comin' here, is she?" asked a man whom I did not know.

"Is that the lady that lives in that house down there?" I asked Robert.

He nodded slowly. "Rosie Woods. Looks like she's coming here." It was said matter-of-factly, with just a trace of curiosity.

The woman was fairly tall and held herself erect, head up. She was attired in a dark-purple dress and a matching hat, adorned with lace and a few small flowers. She wore high heels, making the walk difficult because of the small rocks in the road. Now the porch went quiet. The boys in the yard stopped their talk and watched as she drew near.

She turned between the hedges and came down the small sidewalk, looking straight ahead.

Then she hesitated at the steps. "Good afternoon," she said, her voice low but steady.

Several of the men looked away, but muttered, "Afternoon," as though they weren't sure they should acknowledge her but at the same time not wanting to be unsociable if the others chose to respond.

"Good afternoon, Miz Woods," Robert said.

I added a good afternoon.

Then Robert announced, "Just go on in. It's okay, just go on in."

I was curious, so I went in a few seconds after her. The living room was silent and heavy with the powerful scent of the floral arrangement. Mrs. Helms was seated in the chair nearest the door, gazing up, trying to see who it was.

But the visitor merely nodded, then walked to the coffin where Mr. Helms lay. She stood for a moment in the stillness, nodded her head several times, then turned back toward the door. She stopped by Mrs. Helms.

"I just wanted to come by, 'cause I know he was a decent man," she said, reaching a hand out.

Mrs. Helms began crying anew as she took the hand into both of hers. "He was and I sure do appreciate you comin' by. It means a lot to me; I know Dan would have thought kindly of you."

"Well, he's with the Lord now, you can count on that," Rosie Woods said. "And the Lord's gonna help you get through this, I know."

Then the hands parted and the visitor said, "Well, I just wanted to come by and let you know we was thinking about you."

Mrs. Helms nodded. "Well . . . say a little prayer for us and . . . and be a-comin' back when you can."

Then Rosie Woods went out onto the porch, head erect, gazing straight ahead. With a brief nod to those gathered there, she said, "Afternoon to y'all. I just wanted to come by a moment."

The response this time was more ready, more clear. "Good afternoon," and "Thanks for dropping by."

36

In the years after her husband's death Minnie Belle Helms alternated her lifestyle, staying most of the time with Louise, occasionally coming to Birmingham to visit Millie, and from time to time staying a few days at the old house. But she rarely stayed there at night. Mr. Helms's old garden spots were covered with brown grass from the previous year's overgrowth, and even the little crab-apple tree out back quit bearing.

In 1973 our oldest daughter, Debbie, who was only seventeen, married a tall, strapping young man named Johnny Carpenter, a year older than she was. For a time they lived in the Alexandria area, a few miles south of Wellington. Then in 1984 they bought a mobile home, and Mrs. Helms let them put it in the place where Dan's main garden had been. She began staying at the house more often and even spent many nights there.

One day in 1985 Mrs. Helms and Millie both received letters from the railroad company that operated the tracks out beyond the road, the tracks that ran by Rosie Woods's house.

The company made an offer to buy the house and the adjoining three acres because it was planning to build a cut-off line. The company said if Mrs. Helms refused to sell, they could get a condemnation order and force it. After weeks of debate on the matter, the sale was approved. Millie was contacted because she had put up the $500 down payment on the house and land back in 1957.

But Mrs. Helms didn't want the house torn down. She asked permission to have it moved. The company didn't care. So it was hauled to a parcel of land owned by Louise and Robert. And there it would stay until, years later, it began to fall apart.

Mrs. Helms insisted on leaving the house untouched.

The railroad cut down the big oak tree, cleared the old picket fence off the adjoining property, and plowed under the daffodils.

37

By 1986 Minnie Belle, now in her late eighties, was having more difficulty hearing and seeing. She often spoke haltingly of her husband, referring to him as "your daddy" as she spoke with Louise or Millie.

That same year our daughter Janet, twenty, began dating a young man named Malcolm Morrison, who was an African American. I wasn't happy with the situation, but it was not my decision.

"Just because I wrote about civil rights doesn't mean I want my daughter involved in an interracial marriage," I told her.

But Millie shrugged it off. "You can't live someone else's life for them. All we can do is support her decision. She's still our daughter."

One day in 1987 she told us she was pregnant. We kept that news from Mrs. Helms, as well as everyone else in the family who lived in Wellington. On October 19, 1987, Janet's baby girl was born. She named her Whitney.

I called Debbie to tell her. "Well, I'm coming down to see her," she told me. "And don't worry about it, Dad. It may not be so bad."

One day when the baby was about four months old, and already recognizing all of us, we took her to Wellington to meet the rest of the family. Millie had called Louise and told her. Predictably, the only reaction from my sister-in-law was a drawn out, "Well-ll."

When we arrived at the house on that cool February afternoon, Louise was outside looking at where she wanted to plant flowers. I didn't know what reaction our mixed-race grandchild might have on the family.

But Louise beamed when she saw her, took her from Millie, and paraded her around the yard. Then Robert took his turn, pointing out chickens and rabbits and old, long-necked geese. Then we went inside.

Mrs. Helms was seated on the couch.

"Mother, look who's here," Millie said.

She handed Whitney to Mrs. Helms and sat beside her.

"Well, my goodness, if she don't beat all," she said, the words slow and weak. "She's a fat one, ain't she. I'll bet if your daddy was here he'd put her on his knee and bounce her up and down like a horsy ride. She sure is a chubby thing."

"She sure is," Louise agreed.

Then Millie took the baby back. Mrs. Helms sat gazing at the floor, a perplexed look on her wrinkled face. Her eyes had narrowed and it was clear she was pondering something.

Then she spoke. "Mildred," she said slowly, "is that Debbie's baby?"

"No, Mother, it's Janet's. Her name is Whitney."

"Whitney." She kept her gaze on the floor, still mulling it over. Then:

"That ain't Debbie's baby?"

"No, Mother," Millie said. "Debbie's kids are big now. Dawn is thirteen, and Junior is eleven."

Another long silence. "Well, Mildred, is that baby . . . is that baby colored?"

Before Millie could say anything, Louise cut in patiently: "Momma, it don't matter if the baby is brown or white or whatever color; it's still Jan's baby. And that's all that matters."

"Hmmmp," Minnie grunted, then turned the sound into a brief laugh. "Well, she sure is a fat little thing."

Patsy, Louise's youngest daughter, said, "I'm gonna adopt her one day."

It was surprising to me that a rural Alabama family that had grown up to believe in segregation could so warmly embrace a mixed-race infant. But understanding race and the people of the South was always a little puzzling to me.

Janet and Malcolm married in 1989. So Whitney, and the two who came along later, sister Natalie, and brother Ziggy, would be official members of the family.

It had been me, the liberal reporter . . . no, the liberal damn Yankee reporter, who had been the Doubting Thomas, worrying about reactions. . . .

Minnie Belle Helms died on March 5, 1989. Philip Howell officiated at the funeral. Philip, a Vietnam veteran, had married Joyce Sharpton, Louise's oldest daughter, in 1966. His first wedding to perform was Debbie's marriage to Johnny Carpenter, on December 1, 1973.

After the burial at Bethlehem Baptist Church cemetery, I stood with my sons, Vic, Terry, and Frank Jr., and son-in-law Johnny.

That's when I said I thought I might miss her . . . and when we agreed she had been about the meanest one person we ever knew. But we had to admit that when things had been tough, Dan and Minnie Belle Helms let us come to their home. And when she finally did get so riled that she wanted me out of her house, Louise and Robert had taken us in.

They didn't have much, but they shared it with those in need.

I always wondered why Mrs. Helms had such a volcanic temper. And no one ever came up with a good answer, except that was just her nature. But I figured it might have had something to do with the fact that she was so poor all her life. During the Great Depression just about everybody was poor, and families did without. But after World War II others began to buy cars, get better houses, and enjoy such things as indoor plumbing and air-conditioning. But she

Some of the grandchildren, *from left:* Natalie Sikora, Rachel Sikora, Whitney Sikora, Ashlee Bennett, and *in rear* Kerry Ann Sikora, 1998.

and Dan were still poor, still trying to grub out a living, and never owning a house until 1957.

Minnie Belle and Dan Helms were part of the deep-rooted poverty and the entrenched racial attitudes that defined the lives of thousands of white southerners. But in many ways the slowly changing attitudes of those southerners and their offspring were part of something that marked an end of the Old South as we knew it.

Old times there were not forgotten, but the old ways were being replaced by new values.

In 1991 Millie was diagnosed with lung cancer; she died in December 1992. We buried her beside her mother and father at the Bethlehem Baptist Church cemetery. The graves were overlooked by a giant oak tree that reached well over a hundred feet tall. It was a cold, gray day with blustery winds and falling sleet.

I think of them all often but mostly in early spring, when I see the first yellow daffodils . . .

Editorial Note

Minnie Belle and Dan Helms were born in a segregated society. In their final years they lived much as they had in previous decades. Their lives in northeast Alabama were almost the same in 1970 as they had been in 1935. But their values slowly began to change as did the entire society of the South.

They were my wife's parents, and I had much time to observe their ways: how they talked, what they ate, how they reacted to the civil rights movement. Historic events were changing the social mood in Alabama, as well as in other southern states, but the Helmses and their offspring were in the rear ranks of the change. It had a delayed reaction on them and their adult children and grandchildren, but by the time they died, they had welcomed a mixed-race great-grandchild into their family.

FS
Birmingham
2004